CHALLENGES TO THE
CRIMINAL JUSTICE SYSTEM:

The Perspectives of Community Psychology

Community Psychology Series, Volume 5
American Psychological Association, Division 27

CHALLENGES TO THE CRIMINAL JUSTICE SYSTEM:
The Perspectives of Community Psychology

Community Psychology Series, Volume 5
American Psychological Association, Division 27

Edited by

Theodore R. Sarbin, Ph.D.
Carmel, California

Daniel Adelson, Ph.D., Series Editor
California School of Professional Psychology, Berkeley

HUMAN SCIENCES PRESS
72 Fifth Avenue   3 Henrietta Street
NEW YORK, NY 10011 ● LONDON, WC2E 8LU

Copyright © 1979 by Human Sciences Press
72 Fifth Avenue, New York, New York 10011

Printed in the United States of America
9 987654321

Library of Congress Cataloging in Publication Data

Main entry under title:

Challenges to the criminal justice system.

    (Community psychology series; v. 5)
    Bibliography.
    Includes index.
    1. Criminal justice, Administration of—United States—Addresses, essays, lectures. 2. Social work with delinquents and criminals—United States—Addresses, essays, lectures. 3. Criminal psychology—Addresses, essays, lectures. I. Sarbin, Theodore R. II. Series.
HV8138.C475   364.3   78-32181
ISBN 0-87705-380-4

THE COMMUNITY PSYCHOLOGY SERIES
SPONSORED BY
DIVISION 27 OF THE AMERICAN PSYCHOLOGICAL
ASSOCIATION
SERIES EDITOR, DANIEL ADELSON, PH.D.

The Community Psychology Series has as its central purpose the building of philosophic, theoretical, scientific and empirical foundations for action research in the community and in its subsystems, and for education and training for such action research.

As a publication of the Division of Community Psychology, the series is particularly concerned with the development of community psychology as a sub-area of psychology. In general, it emphasizes the application and integration of theories and findings from other areas of psychology, and in particular the development of community psychology methods, theories, and principles, as these stem from actual community research and practice.

TITLES IN THE COMMUNITY PSYCHOLOGY SERIES

Volume 1: Man as the Measure: The Crossroads, edited by Daniel Adelson

Volume 2: The University and the Urban Crisis, edited by Howard E. Mitchell

Volume 3: Psychological Stress in the Campus Community: Theory, Research and Action, edited by Bernard L. Bloom

Volume 4: Psychology of the Planned Community: The New Town Experience, edited by Donald C. Klein

Volume 5: Challenges to the Criminal Justice System: The Perspectives of Community Psychology, edited by Theodore R. Sarbin

EXECUTIVE COMMITTEE MEMBERS, DIVISION 27 OF THE AMERICAN PSYCHOLOGICAL ASSOCIATION—1978–1979

J. R. Newbrough, Ph.D., President
Julian Rappaport, Ph.D., President-Elect
Murray Levine, Ph.D., Past President
David Stenmark, Ph.D., Secretary-Treasurer
Barbara Dohrenwend, Ph.D., Representative to APA Council
Ira Iscoe, Ph.D., Representative to APA Council
Fred Spaner, Ph.D., Member-at-Large
Sherman James, Ph.D., Member-at-Large
Steven Danish, Ph.D., Member-at-Large
Ann D'Ercole, Student Representative
Meg Gerrard, Newsletter Editor

EDITORIAL BOARD (VOLUMES 1 TO 5)*

Daniel Adelson, Ph.D., General Editor, Volumes 1–5, California School of Professional Psychology, Berkeley
Warren G. Bennis, Ph.D., University of Cincinnati, Ohio
Carl Eisdorfer, Ph.D., Duke University, Durham, North Carolina
Stuart E. Golann, Ph.D., University of Massachusetts, Amherst
Edwin I. Megargee, Florida State University, Tallahassee
Thomas F. Plaut, National Institute of Mental Health, Bethesda, Maryland
Nevitt Sanford, Ph.D., Wright Institute, Berkeley, California
Theodore R. Sarbin, Ph.D., University of California, Santa Cruz
Gary Simpkins, Harvard University, Cambridge, Massachusetts

---

*For Volumes 1 to 5 the Publications Committee members were: Gershen Rosenblum, Ph.D., Chairman; Daniel Adelson, Ph.D., General Editor, Community Psychology Series, Volumes 1–5; Charles Spielberger, Ph.D., former editor, American Journal of Community Psychology; Edison Trickett, Ph.D., former editor, Community Psychology Newsletter; Allen W. Ratcliffe, Ph.D., former editor, Division 27 Newsletter.

Beginning with Volume 6 the Publications Committee members are: Meg Gerrard, Editor, Newsletter and Chair; John C. Glidewell, Editor, American Journal of Community Psychology; Bernard Bloom, Ph.D., General Editor, Community Psychology Series, Volume 6 ff.

Contributors

ROBERT C. FORTHMAN is Associate Professor of Sociology at California State University, Hayward. He worked for a number of years in child welfare and vocational rehabilitation before returning to the University of California at Berkeley to resume graduate study. He was awarded the Doctor of Social Work degree in 1970. Since receiving the D.S.W., he has taught courses in juvenile delinquency, vocational rehabilitation, child welfare, social policy, and other topics. He has contributed to the professional journals and has been involved in research on family supportive services.

GILBERT GEIS is Professor, Program in Social Ecology, University of California, Irvine. He has written extensively on the subject of white-collar crime, including editing *White-Collar Crime,* with Robert F. Meier, published by the Free Press in 1977. He has been President of the American Society of Criminology, Chairman of the Crime and Delinquency section of the Society for the Study of Social Problems, and of the Criminology section of the American Sociological Association.

JOHN MONAHAN is Associate Professor, Program in Social Ecology, University of California, Irvine. He is the author of *The Clinical Prediction of Violent Behavior* and co-author of *Psychology and Community Change.* He is currently President of the

American Psychology-Law Society and has served on the Panel on Legal Issues of the President's Commission on Mental Health, the Panel on Rehabilitation of the National Academy of Sciences, and chaired the Task Force on Psychology in the Criminal Justice System of the American Psychological Association. In 1977, he was a Fellow in Law and Psychology at Harvard Law School.

RAYMOND W. NOVACO is Assistant Professor, Program in Social Ecology, University of California, Irvine. He is the author of *Anger Control: The Development and Evaluation of an Experimental Treatment,* for which he received a research award in 1978 from the International Society for Research on Aggression. His research has been concerned with anger, stress, and cognitive mediational factors.

TONY PLATT is a Research Director of the Institute for the Study of Labor & Economic Crisis, San Francisco, and an Associate Professor of Social Work at California State University, Sacramento. His main academic interest is criminology, which he taught for eight years at the University of California, Berkeley. For the last five years he has been on the Editorial Board of the journal *Crime & Social Justice.* His publications include *The Child Savers, The Politics of Riot Commissions,* and *The Iron Fist & The Velvet Glove.*

RONALD ROESCH received his Ph.D. in community/clinical psychology from the University of Illinois at Urbana–Champaign. His dissertation, which focused on legal and mental health procedures for determining competency to stand trial, was awarded both the Social Issues Dissertation Award and the Consulting Psychology Research Award in 1977. He is currently Assistant Professor of Psychology and Criminology, Simon Fraser University, Burnaby, B.C., Canada. His current research interests include the application of community psychology to criminal justice, psychology and the law, and program evaluations.

THEODORE R. SARBIN's contributions to role theory and a role theory perspective for community psychology have had wide impact. For the past several decades he has also engaged in exploding the myths that underlie many psychological conceptions. Professor Emeritus of Psychology and Criminology at the University of California, Santa Cruz, he now lives and works in Carmel, California.

PHILIP G. ZIMBARDO is Professor of Psychology at Stanford University, where he has taught and conducted research since 1968. He has also taught at Yale University, New York University, Columbia University, and the University of Hawaii. He received the distinguished teaching award in 1975 from the American Psychological Foundation. He has published 10 books and over 70 articles in professional journals. The second edition of *Influencing Attitudes and Changing Behavior* (with E. Ebbesen and C. Maslach) appeared in 1977. The tenth edition of the best selling textbook, *Psychology and Life*, is under Professor Zimbardo's sole authorship.

The subtle power of social situations and institutions to influence and distort individual attitudes, values, and behavior is an underlying theme of his research.

Contents

Preface

Psychologists know how selective are human percep-
tions, how much they depend on prior conceptions, and
how, in turn, they can become self-fulfilling and other-
defining labels. The righteous citizen upholds 'law and
order,' points the finger, and blames those victims whose
presence is an affront to his way of life and sensibilities.

The psychologist often operates within the same 'righteous citizen' myths and even actively rejects challenges
to them. After all, the public pays the service and research
pipers and calls their tunes. Challenges to these are not
inexpensive. There is a price. But how weigh that price
against the price of conceptions of society and myths accepted and unchallenged.

The contributors to this volume brought together by
Theodore R. Sarbin, the scholarly iconoclast, first challenge the myth of the criminal type, then trace the history
of the juvenile justice system as a benevolent approach
which has served to avoid consideration of more basic
social structural factors, and, in three empirical papers:
graphically illustrate the limitations of traditional counseling in working with youth in a poor community; point up
what appears to be the inescapable influence of the system in attempts at 'within system' rehabilitation, with

xi

detailed description of the development of and attempt to evaluate pre-trial diversion measures; and describe the difficulties in pinning responsibility for violence in a large and anonymous corporate structure with suggested strategies for overcoming these. Fundamental however is the need to examine underlying values and assumptions not only of our criminal justice and rehabilitative systems, but also of our corporate and other systems as these influence the attitudes and behavior of those identified with and/or associated with them.

The final paper, by a psychologist whose work has made most clear the readiness of ordinary citizens put in contrived but life-like situations to obey when ordered to be inhuman to fellow man, proposes, nonetheless, that despite and in the face of system factors, man can still choose not to obey and to be human and loving to his fellow man. And here lies the crux of the matter. So that for the community psychologist, the question, most simply put, becomes how to foster individual growth and facilitate the creation of community conditions which make for responsible choice and action.

DANIEL ADELSON

1. The Myth of the Criminal Type*

THEODORE R. SARBIN

In part because scientists have all but eschewed working on problems of crime and justice, the myths that support current institutions tend to perpetuate themselves. It has become the task of research and scholarship to explode myths. In the following article, I have attempted to challenge the myth of the criminal type. As I suggest, belief in the existence of the criminal type is widespread, and even operates as a silent assumption in concurrent theories of crime.

Whether community psychologists perceive their roles in terms of policy advocacy, social reform, community organization, or direct service, at some point they must come face to face with the criminal justice system. The education of most contemporary psychologists gives scant

*An earlier version of this paper was prepared for presentation to the Fellows and guests of the Center for Advanced Studies, Wesleyan University, February 24, 1969, and was privately circulated in a collection entitled *Monday Evening Papers.* Many of the ideas in this paper were generated in interaction with students and faculty colleagues of the School of Criminology, University of California, Berkeley. I mention especially Tim Armistead, Anthony Poveda, Nathan Adler, and the late Joseph Lohman. Kenneth Stein, my co-worker for many years, influenced the development of many of my constructions.

1

attention to criminological and juristic matters. Although relatively sophisticated in so-called mental health ideas, psychologists by and large hold beliefs about the criminal justice system that are not indistinguishable from the general public's beliefs. In the absence of critical information, psychologists must construct their beliefs in the same manner as others, through exposure to the image making of mass media, historical stereotyping, the transmission of folk tales, and the subtle effects of an overpowering ideology.

Understanding of crime and criminals can be advanced by analyzing one outcome of such image-making: the image of the criminal. Because the vagaries of the term "image" might lead to unnecessary semantic confusion, it would be more appropriate to refer to the *social type of the criminal* and the part such a typology plays in a conceptual analysis of the current criminological picture.

The thesis I shall propose depends on the concept of social typing (Sarbin, 1969; Strong, 1943). Everyone has a tendency to categorize in everyday social behavior according to one or more social types: college students, for example, classify each other as athletic types, fraternity types, political types, "hippie" types, etc. (For social types with strong valuational components, the term stereotype is usually employed.) The social type is constructed out of observations where there are departures from the norm, e.g., differences in language, dress, manner, or demeanor. When such noticed differences are related to the "run of attention" of a collective group, the persons who engage in the unique conduct are singled out as a type.

Social types are comprised of sets of beliefs that persons with certain visible and audible characteristics invariably engage in certain forms of behavior. The person who holds such beliefs does not usually question their validity. Racial and ethnic prejudice is one of the outcomes of this common human tendency to sort people into types and to act on the basis of such sorting.

It is important to make clear the distinction between

social and psychological types. Social types are constructed from observations of public behavior. Psychological types are constructed out of chains of inference, measurements, and assessments that are related to *a priori* dimensions, such as introversion, dependency, sympathy, etc. For example, research may show that a certain type as inferred from an ink blot test or personality inventory may be found in a population of law breakers. But to place a particular person in such a psychological typology one must have the results of time-consuming assessments in hand. Placing a person in a social typology, however, is done instantly on the basis of manifest behavior or appearance.

With this brief introductory statement about social types, let me present my argument: Our theories of crime and criminality (and our practices) are influenced by an implicit and unrecognized two-fold typology: that people can be reliably typed as criminal or noncriminal. Many theorists of crime would vehemently reject such a statement as preposterous. The denial is not supported by the facts, however. Many theorists of the crime problem (as well as the general public) begin their thinking from a belief that criminality is a dimension of nature and that people can be readily classified as criminal or noncriminal types. That is to say, such theorists hold a set of unacknowledged premises that regards "the criminal" as the simplistic outcome of a linear process motivated by internal forces, by inimical environmental factors, or both. They tend to conduct a rational inquiry that begins at the wrong place, i.e., at the point of observation of a person who has been convicted of a crime. At this point, the ultimate step in the prolonged legal process, they ask the question: What are the antecedent conditions to the fact that John Smith is a "criminal"? Notwithstanding that the question is raised at the wrong place, the answers have guided three main lines of inquiry: (1) the theory of internal forces, (2) the theory of opportunity structures (the availability of illegitimate means to cultural ends) and (3) the cultural transmission theory. I shall sketch the bare outlines of these perspectives.

THEORY OF INTERNAL FORCES

This perspective has the longest history. The underlying premise is that the criminal is basically defective in some way. In earlier times, the defect was assigned to the germ plasm or the constitution. Lombroso's celebrated work of a century ago (1876) asserted that criminals were constitutionally different from noncriminals. He examined the brains and skulls of convicts and concluded that they had not made it on the evolutionary scale—they were atavisms, throwbacks. Although his results were challenged and later rejected by more careful workers, the idea of the criminal as a degenerate type to be treated as a nonperson, has persisted in popular culture, and in a somewhat attenuated form, in scientific circles.

The site of internal causes was shifted in the first two decades of the 20th century to the "organ of intelligence." This was reflected in a large number of studies carried out with the aid of intelligence tests, first developed by Binet and later adapted by Goddard. The tests were used to assess the intelligence of criminals, i.e., convicted, incarcerated felons. Goddard's conclusion, supported by others, was that the lower I.Q. of prison populations reflected hereditary taints. His conclusions have been challenged on a number of grounds, one of which was the nonrepresentativeness of items in the early intelligence tests that biased the results against persons who had not been to school.

The mental deficiency notion gave way to mental illness as a causal force. All criminals could be described as mentally ill, because if they were mentally healthy they would not be criminals. Proponents of mental illness causality could support this circularity by producing evidence from the life histories of convicted felons to show inimical early childhood experiences, deprivation of love and affection, late weaning, poor superego formation, improper toilet training habits, and unresolved Oedipus conflicts. Unfortunately for the theory, the same characteristics were found in noncriminal samples.

Although the internal forces theories have not fared well, their sticky persistence tells us something of value, i.e., at least for the past 100 years, criminologists have sought data to support the notion of a criminal type. Because they focused on a restricted and perhaps unrepresentative sample of law-breakers, i.e., convicted felons, they could find some support for their hypothesis. An important question was overlooked: Was the belief in criminal types an operative feature of the prevailing value system that selected out certain types to be arrested, accused, convicted, and imprisoned? Stated in another way, were the unrecognized beliefs of the theorists matched by the unacknowledged biases of law enforcement officers and judicial officials?

THE OPPORTUNITY STRUCTURE THEORY

The most frequently employed theory of crime is associated with the anomie concept of Merton (1957). It has been used by a large number of sociologically-oriented theorists to account for all kinds of deviance. The basic paradigm is a simple one: a person is a criminal because he has been denied access to legitimate means for achieving culturally-shared goals, therefore turns to illegitimate means, i.e., crime. This conception, like the first, contains a hidden premise in the form of an unrecognized belief about law-breakers. The theory, as presented and used, makes assumptions that are not continuous with sophisticated observations in that it relies exclusively on official police reports and court records. A bias is immediately inserted by relying on official statistics. Although in theory, police are employed to enforce all the laws, their ratings of efficiency are based on clearing complaints of certain types, such as murder, rape, robbery, assault, burglary, larceny, and auto theft. Because these offenses occur primarily in disorganized ghetto cultures, the poor, the uneducated, the alien, and the wretched of the earth become the significant statistics. By limiting himself to such reports and records, a theorist could only construct a paradigm that crime occurs where legitimate means to cultural goals are denied.

However, a review of the literature on middle class delinquency and white-collar crime leaves little doubt that law violations are not uncommon among persons to whom legitimate means are not denied. The classic work that clearly demonstrates the bias in explanations of crime as a class-linked phenomenon is Sutherland's study of white-collar crime (1949). His analysis was directed to 70 major corporations. He was concerned with several kinds of violations: restraint of trade, misrepresentation in advertising, patent infringement, trademarks and copyrights, and unfair labor practices. Everyone of the corporations had one or more unfavorable decisions (verdicts of guilty), the maximum number of unfavorable decisions being 50, the average being 14 per corporation. Although by standard definitions, nearly 80 percent of the complaints could be classified as crimes, most of the violations were handled as quasi-crimes, by administrative boards.

The Watergate experience, and the criminal acts of corporate officers (Geis & Meier, 1977) should also be cited as evidence that illegal acts are performed by persons to whom legitimate means are open.

Understanding the concept of crime, then, requires more than a belief in the means-end doctrine, the belief that people engage in illegal activities because they are denied access to legitimate means of satisfying their wants. The conclusion is warranted that in the formulation and the development of the theory, the idea of the criminal type appeared as a hidden or disguised premise. The theorists of the means-end doctrine were probably subtly influenced by the same beliefs that were expressed in undisguised form in the propositions of W. Berge, an official of the antitrust division in the Department of Justice. In arguing against the employment of criminal prosecutions under the Sherman antitrust laws, he said,

> While civil penalties may be as severe in their financial effects as criminal penalties, yet they do not involve the stigma that attends indictment and conviction. Most of the defendants in antitrust cases are not criminals in the usual sense. There is no inherent reason why anti-trust enforcement requires branding them as such (Berge, 1940, p. 111)

Unlike most theorists of crime, this government official was outspoken in expressing his belief that there is a criminal type and a noncriminal type.[1]

CULTURAL TRANSMISSION MODEL

The focus of the third model is not so much on the antecedents to deviant conduct, but rather on the persistence of criminal groups over time, their inner dynamics, their recruitment practices, etc. It is more concerned with occupational sociology and in this context is neutral in regard to the existence of criminal types. However, like the other models, attention has not been directed to the part played by the agencies of social control and justice in the cultural transmission of law-violating behavior.

[1]An account of the greatest antitrust conspiracy in the history of the United States (Herling, 1962) is appropriate here. Notwithstanding that the characters in the drama were hard-working leaders of business and civic affairs, respected in their communities, "their activities in the electrical conspiracies frequently took on the color of a gangster movie, with a cast made up of captains of industry" (p. ix).

The most widely-cited studies illustrative of the cultural transmission theory are those of Shaw and McKay (1942). Working in the late 1920's and early 1930's, they analyzed Chicago's public records by census tracts and noted the geographical distribution of social pathology, including recorded crime and delinquency. The greatest frequencies were in those interstitial zones of the city, i.e., those residential areas that had large numbers of rooming houses, cheap hotels, substandard housing, and other indicators of slum life.

The ecological method was used in other large cities and the same conclusions reached, i.e., that the social organization of the slum provided the potential recruits to the criminal system with opportunities for associating with and learning from successful criminals. An outstanding finding was that the same relative frequencies of crime and delinquency held for the slum areas regardless of the wave of immigrants residing there at any particular time. In short, it did not matter whether the Irish, the Poles, the Italians, or the blacks (one group replacing the group before it) were residents, the rates of reported crime and delinquency remained high. One explanation was that the criminal culture was somehow transmitted from one ethnic group to the next. In the idiom of the present analysis (and to preview a later argument), I would suggest another explanation, one that would take into account the constancy of the belief systems of those charged with the responsibility for maintaining order and enforcing laws. I would suggest that police institutions held and transmitted beliefs about impoverished immigrants being actual or potential members of "dangerous classes." The belief that some classes of persons were "dangerous" guided the search for suspects and for preventive attention by policy and other agents of social control. Laws were broken by many citizens for many reasons: those suspects who fit the concurrent social type of the criminal were most likely to become objects of police suspicion and of judicial decision making.

MYTH MAKING

I have sketched three prevailing perspectives on the nature of the criminal and I have alluded to the weaknesses in these formulations. I propose, now, that the perpetrators and the users of these notions are guilty of myth making. The criminal as a social type is a myth (as is, incidentally, the law-abiding citizen as a social type). When I assert that the criminal is a myth, I am suggesting that the theorists have begun their cognitive work from a tacit and false premise: to wit, that there exists in modern society a type of person who cannot or will not live by the rules of his society. Furthermore, given the opportunity and other ecological conditions, he will inevitably engage in violations of the law.

To support this rather bold contention that the so-called criminal type is a lively fiction, it is necessary to employ the distinction between efficient causes and formal causes, or as Lemert puts it, between original and effective causes (1967). Making use of this distinction, we move from the general and footless question: what causes crime? to two specific questions that, in principle, are answerable. The first question is directed to the efficient cause, i.e., what are the conditions antecedent to the performance of an act that violates a law? (A moment's reflection leads us to the conclusion that the subordinate clause is unnecessary, we need only know the conditions that elicit a particular act. Whether the act violates a law or not is a matter of *posthoc* evaluation.) The second question is directed to the formal cause, What are the conditions antecedent to classifying a person as a criminal. In isolating these two questions, I have pointed up an important observation made repeatedly by sophisticated students of crime: that the efficient cause (performance of an unlawful act) and the formal cause (being classified and labeled as a criminal) are not related in a transitive way. That is to say, not all persons who violate laws are labeled criminals.

The answers to the first question are the answers to all the questions of psychology, or, how to account for individual differences in conduct. Suffice it to say here that nearly everyone violates some ordinance, civil regulation, or penal code in the business of meeting life's contingencies. Everyone can remember committing delicts, acts that clearly violate laws, some of which are classified as felonies, punishable in some states by imprisonment of one year or more. Especially instructive is the often-cited study by Wallerstein and Wyle (1947) entitled "Our Law-abiding Law-breakers." They distributed questionnaires (with guarantees of anonymity) to nearly 1,700 respondents, mostly from New York City. The questionnaires contained 49 offenses that carried sentences of not less than one year. The sample was considered to be roughly proportional to the population in terms of socioeconomic characteristics. Of this sample, 99 percent indicated that they had committed at least one offense. The mean number of offenses was 18. None of the sample had been classified as a criminal. Among the offenses listed on the questionnaire were such classes of items as malicious mischief, disorderly conduct, robbery, bribery, criminal libel, falsification and fraud, perjury, indecency, assault, health law violations, etc.[2]

The universality of undetected and unlabeled violations of the law has been documented repeatedly. Porterfield (1946) reported on the remembered juvenile offenses of college students. The types of offenses were of the same degree of seriousness as those of a sample of juvenile court cases.

That the commission of illegal acts is not restricted to lower class youth is amply demonstrated in a study by Short and Nye (1957). Instead of relying on court and police statistics, they submitted questionnaires to 3000

[2]The Summary of the Presidential Commission's report provides supporting documentation. See *The Challenge of Crime in a Free Society: A Report by the President's Commission on Law Enforcement and Administration of Justice.* Washington, D.C., U.S. Government Printing Office, 1967.

high school students, with a guarantee of anonymity. Their findings revealed the high incidence of unlawful acts and, further, the lack of differential incidence by socioeconomic status. Sarbin and Stein confirmed these findings (1968). Data obtained from a *Delinquency Check List* (Kulik, Stein, & Sarbin, 1968), which was administered anonymously, showed that socioeconomic status and scores on the *Delinquency Check List* were unrelated.

I have already alluded to Sutherland's study of white-collar crime. I might also mention that embezzlers, check forgers, confidence men, and tax evaders are not drawn from the impoverished classes. No figures are available, but the number of detected and undetected law violations committed by middle-class persons must be astronomical.

The conclusion is warranted that law violation is a rather common happening in any stratum of society. Therefore, as I suggested before, the study of efficient causes of crime demands inquiries that will provide answers to most of the persisting questions of behavior analysis, especially in such areas as moral development, the acquisition of techniques for the delay of gratification, the sanctioning properties of shame and guilt, the assessment of risk, the choice between instrumental and ritual satisfaction of wants, the short and long range costs and rewards of conformity, impulse control, tension and time-binding and many more. In short, the study of the antecedents to law breaking will involve us in the study of individual differences, especially those variables that have been identified and employed by students of cognition and of social psychology.

FORMAL CAUSES

The second question—the question of formal causes—requires an excursion into the study of those social organizations that have been allocated the power and responsibility for assigning the label of criminal to law violators. Although it is a matter of common knowledge that only a small number of law violations is detected and reported, the nature of police statistics has not allowed for complete documentation. For example, in the five years covered by the Cambridge-Somerville Youth Study, the researchers recorded 6416 violations, of which only 95 were officially entered as complaints, or less than 1.5 percent (Murphy, Shirley, & Witmer, 1946).

Over a decade ago, Ennis (1967) provided data and interpretation that supported the proposition that the official designation "criminal" is applied to an infinitesimal proportion of law violators. In a survey of 10,000 households, a staff of interviewers turned up 3400 incidents that were related to crimes of violence and to property crimes. Such self-incriminating violations as illegal gambling, narcotics violations, and illegal abortions were not subject to inquiry. Almost 2100 of these incidents were verified as crimes by lawyers and policemen. The first step in the attrition process was in notifying the police. More than half the incidents were not reported to the police. Of those crimes reported to the police 77 percent were investigated, of which 75 percent were labeled as crime by the investigating officers. Police made arrests in 80 percent of the cases that they had labeled as crimes. Of these, 42 percent were brought to trial. The alleged offender was convicted in 52 percent of the cases of those who were tried.

In this carefully conducted study, which was designed to obtain information on unlawful victimization of a restricted sort, the label "criminal" would be applied only to 50 out of 2100 potential candidates, or a ratio of 1:42.

A fruitful field for social psychological study is the decision-making processes in the steps of the legal process. What events and beliefs led the police not to investigate a victim's complaints; or not to label a victimization as a crime; and led to turning up and arresting suspects in some cases and not in others? Only one-fifth of those arrested go to trial. What influenced the district attorney to bring some cases to trial and not others? These and other questions remain to be answered.

Taking our cue from the steps in the legal process, then, a person, to be officially classified as a criminal, must be subjected to a series of social valuations by relevant others. Each valuation may result in a different status being conferred upon him. First, agents of social control (usually the police) may attach the label *suspect* to an individual who may or may not have committed a particular violation. Second, the same agents may confirm the application of the label by an arrest. Third, the individual may be charged with committing a crime, i.e., labeled as *defendant* through the complicated accusatory process of the magisterial institution. Fourth, he may be tried and found guilty and assigned the status of *felon* and sentenced. Finally, he may be incarcerated in a penal institution and labeled *convict* or *inmate* or *prisoner*. (It is important to note that with rare exceptions the pool of subjects for students of the "criminal mind" have been persons in the final status of the legal process, inmates of penal institutions.) The transition from the status of suspect to the ultimate status of convict occurs along a continuum that might be described as status degradation, as moving from the status of person to the status of nonperson via several way stations. At each way station, only a small number are funneled into the next, lower status. The immediate and remote effects of status degradation as a generator of deviant conduct are far reaching. In another place I have shown how the efficient cause of deviant conduct may be understood as a function in part of the downward transvaluation of social identity, a direct outcome of status degradation.

To get at the formal causes, the behavioral scientist must uncover those personal and organizational factors that operate to reduce the original pool of undifferentiated violators to a small pool of convicts, i.e., "criminals" who, as it turns out, do not share the demographic characteristics of middle- and upper-class citizens. To be sure, there have been variations in specific characteristics of those who make up the class "criminals." That is to say, at least for the past 100 years, the general characteristic of "non-middle class" (including non-upper class) has described most of the prison population, but specific ethnic characteristics have changed over the years. At one point in time, Irish immigrants were overrepresented in official police records and in the prison population, at another time, immigrants from Central Europe were overrepresented, and at the present time, individuals who are black are overrepresented.

To put the conclusion more bluntly, membership in the class "law breakers" *is not* distributed according to economic or social status, but membership in the class "criminals" *is* distributed according to social or economic status.

The funneling effect will occur in any case; suspects may be released for lack of evidence, the backlog of cases in the district attorney's office may be a factor in dismissing some potential defendants, etc. Notwithstanding, the social class bias in the funneling effect is a compelling observation. To account for the disproportionate number of lower class and black prisoners, I propose that the agents of law enforcement and justice engage in decision making against a backcloth of belief that people can be readily classified into two types, criminal and noncriminal.

To support this assertion, I refer again to the common human tendency to make use of social or folk types (Sarbin, 1969). A social typology is formed out of the needs and purposes of an individual or group. Cues in the form of public behavior, dress, health habits, speech, skin color, demeanor, residence, accent, etc., are matched against the defining criteria of the social type. Where the typology is a two-fold one, criminal and noncriminal, those persons who fit the defining criteria of the "criminal type" are more likely to be assigned the successively degraded statuses of suspect, defendant, felon, and convict.

It remains now to describe the conditions that made it possible to specify the criteria for sorting people into criminal and noncriminal types. In order to understand the employment of this typology, I must digress and review the conditions that produced in the nineteenth century (and probably earlier) the concept "dangerous classes" and, concomitantly, the police institution.

THE CONCEPT OF THE DANGEROUS CLASSES

To understand the origin and use of the concept "dangerous classes," it is necessary first to look at the concept of danger. Like the analysis of any complex phenomenon, the analysis of danger is helped along by a semantic study (Sarbin, 1967). This is especially true if we take a backward glance at the metaphorical beginnings. Words, as we know, are molded and sustained to fill the needs of human beings to communicate with each other. We might expect the origins of the word "danger" to be related to physicalistic conceptions because of its current use in denoting physical objects and events that might damage property or injure people. Surprisingly, this is not the case. The term seems to have been shaped out of linguistic roots that signified *relative position in a social structure,* a relationship between roles on a power dimension. The root is found in Latin in a derivative of *dominium,* meaning lordship or sovereignty. According to the Oxford English Dictionary, the word came into Middle English through Old French and carried the meaning of "power of a Lord or master, jurisdiction; power to dispose of, or to hurt or harm; especially in phrases such as 'in a person's danger,' within his power or at his mercy; sometimes meaning specifically in his debt or under obligation." Following the implication of this brief etymological analysis leads us into the conception of danger as a symbol denoting relative power in a social organization.

If we revive the older meaning of danger as *dominium,*

then, as a relationship between positions in a social structure based on relative power, an interesting network of conceptions emerges. This network includes the notion of role-system, the reciprocity of rights and duties, the relationship between power and responsibility, the shaping of social identity through placement in the role system, and, not the least important, the possibility of the transvaluation of social identity through economic, political, and legal practices. When the transvaluation occurs in a downward direction, a point is reached where the individual is faced with the choice of accepting the identity of a nonperson, a brute, or engaging in instrumental behavior that radically alters the social system and reverses the *dominium*, the power relationship, thus affording him a more acceptable social identity. Such a solution, of course, is perceived as danger by those whose grant of power is thus challenged. The employment of this conception helps in understanding social disturbances and riots, the conduct that was in part the basis for coining the concept "dangerous classes."

From this preliminary statement about the concept of danger, the argument is straightforward. Those persons or groups that threaten the existing power structure are dangerous. In any historical period, to identify an *individual* whose status is that of member of the "dangerous classes," the label "criminal" has been handy. As I have said before, the typological construct, criminal, is not used to classify the performers of all legally defined delicts, only those whose position in the social structure qualifies them for membership in the dangerous classes.

The concept of dangerous classes was developed in the United States during the period of rapid social and technological change. The period following the Civil War witnessed the beginning of an acute conflict between the traditional values of the agrarian way of life and the lifestyles of the industrial city. Young people left the farms and villages to seek their fortunes in the cities. Documentation is ample that this migration resulted in shifts in social identities that had been supported by the stable family group to social identities that were reflections of the fluctuating, faceless, ambiguous social organization of the metropolis.

This inmigration was swollen by the millions of peasant-immigrants from central and Southern Europe. The failure of the cities to accommodate its housing, sanitation, and other public services to the transplanted peasant values of the hordes of incoming immigrants resulted in the creation of subcultures of poverty with their associated slums, disease, and disorder.

A review of political history shows that the power structure of the United States remained in the hands of those with traditional agrarian sentiments. They distrusted the urban dwellers, especially those who did not fit the conformant image of the Anglo-Saxon protestant. Those with power had subscribed to the concept of the manifest destiny of the Anglo-Saxon people. According to one protagonist, America would become "a vast theatre on which to work out the grand experiment of Republican government, under the auspices of the Anglo-Saxon race" (quoted in Blum, et al., 1963, p. 261). This political conception, among others, such as the rise of the labor union movement, paved the way for categorizing the "foreigner" as a class or type fundamentally different from native Americans. The following declamation by Josiah Strong (1885), an evangelical leader and social reformer, illustrates the force of this public policy.

> It is not necessary to argue ... that the two great needs of mankind ... are, first, a pure, spiritual Christianity, and, second, civil liberty.... These are the forces, which ... have contributed most to the elevation of the human race, and they must continue to be, in the future, the most efficient ministers to its progress. It follows, then, that the Anglo-Saxon, as the great representative of these two ideas, the depositary of these two great blessings, sustains peculiar relations to the world's future, is divinely com-

> missioned to be, in a peculiar sense, his brother's
> keeper. . . . It seems to me that God, with infinite
> wisdom and skill, is training the Anglo-Saxon race for
> an hour sure to come in the world's future. (p. 213)

With this polarization of attitudes fostered by those who
lived and breathed the doctrine of the manifest destiny of
the Anglo-Saxon race, and with the recognition of the
growing threat of urban thought-ways, the categorizing of
immigrants and other strangers as potentially dangerous
was an easy step. With the increase in reported crimes
that followed ineluctably the disorganization and exploitation in the cities, the dangerous classes were regarded
as breeders and developers of criminals.

In 1872, Charles Loring Brace, eager for the establishment of extended social services, made note of the association of crime and violence with being impoverished and
foreign-born.

> Thousands are the children of poor foreigners, who
> have permitted them to grow up without school, ed-
> ucation, or religion. All the neglect and bad educa-
> tion and evil example of a poor class tend to form
> others, who, as they mature, swell the ranks of ruffi-
> ans and criminals. So, at length, a great multitude of
> ignorant, untrained, passionate, irreligious boys and
> young men are formed, who become the "dangerous
> class" of our city. They form the "Nineteenth-Street
> Gangs," the young burglars and murderers, the gar-
> roters and rioters, the thieves and flash-men, the "re-
> peaters" and ruffians, so well known to all who know
> this metropolis. (p. 101)

Another alarmed observer had no qualms about conjoin-
ing immigrants with criminality when he wrote:

> In the poorer quarters of our great cities may be
> found huddled together the Italian bandit and the

bloodthirsty Spaniard, the bad man from Sicily, the Hungarian, Croatian and the Pole, the Chinaman and the Negro, the cockney Englishman, the Russian and the Jew, with all the centuries of hereditary hate back of them. . . . We claim to be a rich, a prosperous city and yet we cannot afford to employ enough policemen to keep thieves and burglars out of our houses and thugs and robbers from knocking us on the head as we walk on our streets. (Brown, 1907 p. 832)

Connecting the status of immigrant with that of criminal was the chief argument of the Native American party, a pre-Civil War political organization. From that period into the present century, newspapers and other media carried statistics to show the disproportionate rates of crime and pauperism for the foreign-born and the children of foreign-born when compared with native born whites (read Anglo-Saxon).

Writing in the *Popular Science Monthly* Fisher (1896) argued for the deleterious effects of unrestricted immigration. He supported his arguments with quotes from Washington, Jefferson, and Madison, and also presented statistics from the census of 1890. Using ratios of prisoners to population, he noted 882 native white prisoners per million, 1747 foreign whites per million, and 3250 Negroes per million. He was constrained to add an explanatory paragraph about the Negro rate:

The negro, though born to the soil, is in every sense an alien, and if we wish to see how much crime is due to our various experiments in importing foreign populations we have only to connect the negro ratio of crime with the foreign white ratio and compare them with the native ratio. . . . (p. 627)

This writer was one of many who drew the inference that crime and pauperism are necessary correlates of being a foreigner. From such reasoning he developed the thesis

that immigrants, especially impoverished ones, constituted a danger to the America of our "rugged ancestors."
As I indicated earlier, census reports and police records
only tell us of some of the characteristics of persons who
have been processed through the police, magisterial, and
penal institutions. Such records are silent in regard to the
characteristics of law-breakers who have not been processed through these fallible institutions.

I have quoted these writers and pamphleteers to illustrate how the social and linguistic conditions set the stage
for the formulation of the dichotomous typology, the
criminal and the noncriminal. Being a foreigner, being
poor, being black could lead to a person's being classified
as a member of the ambiguously defined "dangerous
class." Since the concepts danger and criminality were
regarded as virtually identical, as being close neighbors in
cognitive space, when a person was seen as dangerous he
was likely to be seen also as an exemplar of the criminal
type. On the other hand, a person who could be classified
as a native Anglo-Saxon type was not likely to be cast as
a criminal type.

I have argued that the criminal type can best be regarded as a myth. Unlike a labeled metaphor or a simile,
the myth contains directions for action within itself. Thus
when a police officer in the course of his patrol duties
encounters an individual, the concept "danger" and associated concept "criminal" have a high access-ordering.
The policeman's efficiency rating, if not his survival, depends upon an accurate assessment of the "danger" potential of the other. The typology stands ready to provide
him with a means for quick assessment.

A number of reports have been issued that illustrate the
process of social typing in police work. One widely quoted
study was carried out by Piliavin and Briar (1964). At first
hand, they studied police encounters with juveniles. The
police officers who were the targets of the study were
members of a juvenile detail, who had wide latitude in the
disposition of boys encountered in the course of patrolling

neighborhoods with high crime rates. The decision to cite or arrest a boy in the absence of *flagrante delicto* was based on an implicit typology of "character." The cues employed to sort boys into types for dispensing on-the-spot justice included group affiliations, age, race, grooming, dress, and demeanor. "Older juveniles, members of known delinquent gangs, Negroes, youths with well-oiled hair, black jackets and soiled denims or jeans (the presumed uniforms of 'tough' boys) and boys who in their interactions with officers did not manifest . . . appropriate signs of respect" received the more severe dispositions.

In addition to the conclusions drawn from empirical studies, the folk lore of police administration endorses the belief that a criminal type does exist. A police manual asserts: "The majority of persons who have criminal tendencies seek similar companions. These groups become clannish, developing their own special language, hair style and clothing preferences, and districts of residence" (Bristow, 1957, p. 21). That persons with noncriminal tendencies are also clannish, conformant in clothing, and hair style is not proposed. The job for the patrolman is to acquire proficiency in noting cues that characterize the so-called criminal type. The thrust of police training manuals, as well as informal inservice training, is to sensitize the patrolman to be suspicious of any and all deviations from his baseline of observation, a condition that inevitably leads to the development of the cognitive construct labeled by Skolnick "the symbolic assailant" (1967). The concept is strengthened by authoritative statements in the manual, such as "The number of officers killed each year while approaching motorists or pedestrians for routine interrogations indicates that the patrolman should assume every [*sic*] person he encounters may be armed. Many experienced officers carry a small pistol in their jacket or trouser pocket. This type of weapon may be held in the hand, concealed in the pocket or by a note book, and is ready instantly for use should the situation require it" (Bristow 1957, pp. 15–16). The cognitive work involved when the patrolman conducts a field interrogation is admittedly complex and probabilistic and is reflected in the following excerpts from the training manual already cited (Bristow, 1957). Such complexity is reduced by creating and using the simplistic nonprobabilistic typology: criminal and noncriminal.

> Experience gained from frequent field interrogations will give the officer an indication as to what constitutes normal compliance for various types of subjects. Generally the irate, annoyed, sarcastic, or uncooperative attitude might be expected from a subject who is in advanced years or who may be considered an affluent citizen. Such an attitude on the part of a juvenile or young adult, however, indicates that the subject may have something to conceal and wishes to eliminate further conversation or contact with the officer. (p. 35)

> Occasionally the subject will exhibit an overly friendly attitude, punctuating his conversation with an excess of "no, sir" or "yes, sir" replies. Subjects who tend to be overly solicitous should be regarded with suspicion, as they may be trying *too hard* to convince the officer of their good intentions. Further interrogation may reveal that the subject uses the word "sir" in excess because of prior prison training. (p. 36)

The myth of the criminal type, like other myths, lends itself to the self-fulfilling prophesy. Since men and women respond to the constructions they place upon occurrences, the immediate and remote consequences of their conduct is determined by their constructions, i.e., by the meanings assigned to the occurrences. The self-fulfilling prophesy, as Merton took pains to point out, begins from a *false* definition of the situation. That is, the definition is not constructed out of empirical events and objects, but out of other considerations, such as the degree of risk attendant upon assigning a benign meaning to an event.

But the false definition calls out conduct on the part of the actor (e.g., the police officer) and reciprocally on the part of the other (e.g., the suspect) that makes the definition come true. As Merton has declared: "the specious validity of the self-fulfilling prophesy perpetuates a reign of error. For the prophet will cite the actual course of events as proof that he was right from the very beginning" (1957).

Although recent analyses of police practices show clearly the operation of the typology and its associated mythology, it would be a mistake to infer from my remarks that the police are inherently evil or stupid, or both. The police institution has arisen in the United States in the context of other institutions, legal, economic, and political, among others. These interrelated institutions provide the values and the supporting beliefs for the concept of the dangerous classes. If these other institutions were to be analyzed with the same thoroughness as the institution of the police, I am sure the same kind of typology would be found and with the same mythological implications.

It would not be correct to infer that I believe a conspiracy exists between police, prosecutors, judges, and prison officials to imprison and degrade impoverished and poorly-educated people. The more acceptable inference is that political, economic, and social events have been instrumental in creating a set of beliefs and an organizational structure that have been only partially successful in administering social justice.

It is too easy for students of society to polarize their attitudes and take a position that is either hostile to contemporary police institutions or hostile to the idea of change in the structure and function of peace-keeping agencies. Rather than placing blame for inadequacies and injustices in the present crisis, my analysis is intended to show that prevailing police and magisterial practices are historically-rooted in an invalid typology. The next step for social policy-makers is no small one: to change beliefs that crime and the underclass are necessarily conjoined.

CONCLUSION

The concluding statements are written from a humanistic viewpoint to account for an element of moral indignation that shows through the analysis. As I have argued, the formal cause of crime is to be found in the practices of those persons who have the power to arrest and detain, to accuse and to pass sentence. To the degree that their actions are governed by demonstrably mythical concepts, to a commensurate degree are the canons of democratic social justice violated. One such mythical concept is the criminal type.

If, as W. B. Yeats wrote, "science is the critique of myths," then it is appropriate to the role of the social scientist to explode the myth. Once this occurs, social policy makers can demand alternate practices in the enforcement of law and the administration of justice. We must not minimize the problems inherent in such an undertaking. The targets of the myth—degraded men and women—have created their own belief systems about agents of the power structure. They, too, must recognize to what extent their conduct is governed by myth and to what extent by objective conditions. In this interactive way, the exposing of reciprocal myths can serve the cause of democratic social justice. But I must emphasize that those organized institutions of social control and those less organized segments of the population whose conduct is the object of such institutions now form a system. To change the prevailing beliefs of two or more collectivities that through historical processes have become adversaries will require much from all of us. Because we must deal concurrently with several subsystems, the job is beset with many difficulties. Success will not come overnight, and will *not* follow from technological improvements in surveillance, detection, and control procedures. If we succeed at all, it will be because we will have influenced social policy makers to view crime as a set of human relations problems closely tied to the nature of social organization rather than as a problem related to human wickedness or to the expression of innate evil. If such an alternate conception is adopted, humanists and social scientists stand ready to apply their knowledge and skills in the interests of social justice.

Because the argument has led me into a conclusion that conjoins several concepts: danger, degradation, crime, and police, I am constrained again to caution the reader against constructing a simple causality proposition: that individual police officers are the villains in the social drama. Many, if not all, of the antecedent conditions that produced the widespread belief in the criminal type also produced the institution of the police. As Skolnick (1967) and others have concluded, the development of the *role of the policeman* may be accounted for with the same analytical concepts as the development of any other occupational role. When a student looks at processes of recruitment, training, kinds of actual and potential rewards for service, the nature of the actions that are assessed as proper by fellow-officers and superiors, the psychological isolation and geographical separation of the policeman from his clients, and so on, the interrelationships of our social institutions stand out.

The solution to one of the most acute problems in contemporary society lies neither in the practice of some potential clients who angrily demean the police nor in the practice of some police who degrade their clients with insulting slurs and threats. Rather the solution is to be found in efforts to break up the systemic binds whose origins are in historical processes, not in human nature.

REFERENCES

Berge, W. Remedies available to the government under the Sherman Act. *Law and Contemporary Problems,* 1940, 7, iii.

Blum, J. M., Cotton, B., Morgan, E. S., Schlesinger, A. M.,

Jr., Stampp, K. M., & Woodward, C. Vann. *The national experience.* New York: Harcourt, Brace and World, 1963.

Brace, C. L. *The dangerous classes of New York.* New York: Wynkoop and Hallenbeck, 1872.

Bristow, A. P. *Field interrogation.* Springfield, Ill.: Charles C Thomas, 1957.

Brown, J. E. The increase of crime in the United States. *The Independent,* 1907, 832–833.

Ennis, P. H. Crimes, victims, and the police. *Transaction,* 1967, 36–44.

Fisher, S. G. Crime and immigration. *Popular Science Monthly,* 1896, *49,* 625–630.

Geis, G., & Meier, R. *White collar crime: Offences in business, politics, and the professions.* New York: Free Press, 1977.

Herling, J. *The great price conspiracy: The story of the antitrust violations in the electrical industry.* Washington, D.C.: Robert B. Luce, 1962.

Kulik, J. A., Stein, K. B., & Sarbin, T. R. Dimensions and patterns of adolescent antisocial behavior. *Journal of Consulting and Clinical Psychology,* 1968, *32,* 375–382.

Lemert, E. M. *Human deviance, social problems, and social control.* Englewood Cliffs, N.J.: Prentice-Hall, 1967.

Lombroso, C. *L'uomo delinquente in rapporto all'antropologia, alla giurisprudenza ed alle discipline carcerarie,* 3 vols., Turin: Bocca, 1876.

Merton, R. K. *Social theory and social structure.* Glencoe: Free Press, 1957.

Murphy, F., Shirley, M., & Witmer, H. L. The incidence of hidden delinquency. *American Journal of Orthopsychiatry,* 1946, *16,* 686–696.

Piliavin, I., & Briar, J. S. Police encounters with juveniles. *American Journal of Sociology,* 1964, *70,* 206–214.

Porterfield, A. L. *Youth in trouble.* Fort Worth: Leo Potishman Foundation, 1946.

Sarbin, T. R. The dangerous individual: An outcome of social identity transformations. *British Journal of Criminology,* 1967, *7,* 285–295.

Sarbin, T. R. On the distinction between social roles and social types, with special reference to the hippie. *American Journal of Psychiatry,* 1969, *125,* 1024–1031.

Sarbin, T. R., & Scheibe, K. E. *The Transvaluation of Social Identity,* unpublished manuscript, 1969.

Shaw, C., & McKay, H. *Juvenile delinquency and Urban Areas.* Chicago: University of Chicago Press, 1942.

Short, J., & Nye, F. I. Reported behavior as a criterion of deviant behavior. *Social Problems,* 1957, *5,* 207–213.

Skolnick, J. H. *Justice without trial: Law enforcement in a democratic society.* New York: Wiley, 1967.

Strong, J. *Our country.* New York: Baker and Taylor, 1885.

Strong, S. Social types in a minority group: Formulation of a method. *American Journal of Sociology,* 1943, *48,* 563–573.

Sutherland, E. H. *White collar crime.* New York: Holt, 1949.

Wallerstein, J., & Wyle, C. J. Our law-abiding lawbreakers. *Probation,* 1947, *25,* 107–112.

2. The Triumph of Benevolence: The Origins of the Juvenile Justice System in the United States*

TONY PLATT

It is now a commonplace observation that the first step in social change is the recognition that an existing institution is but one arrangement for dealing with social problems, and is not the only one. In directing our attention to the origins of the juvenile justice system, Platt sensitizes us to the conclusion that the present arrangement for controlling the unwanted behavior of juveniles is but one possible arrangement. He underscores the observation that current institutions have become counterproductive as deterrents and as rehabilitators.

TRADITIONAL PERSPECTIVES ON JUVENILE JUSTICE

The modern system of crime control in the United States has many roots in penal and judicial reforms that were undertaken at the end of the 19th century. Contemporary programs which we commonly associate with the "war on poverty" and the "great society" can be traced in numerous instances to the programs and ideas of the

*Published by permission of the author. Copyright 1976 Tony Platt. This is a shortened version of an essay which appeared in Richard Quinney (Ed.), *Criminal Justice in America* (Little, Brown & Co., 1974).

19th century reformers who helped to create and develop probation and parole, the juvenile court, strategies of crime prevention, the need for education and rehabilitative programs in institutions, the indeterminate sentence, the concept of "half-way" houses, and "cottage" systems of penal organization.

The creation of the juvenile court and its accompanying services is generally regarded by scholars as one of the most innovative and idealistic products of the age of reform. It typified the "spirit of social justice," and, according to the National Crime Commission, represented a progressive effort by concerned reformers to alleviate the miseries of urban life and to solve social problems by rational, enlightened, and scientific methods.[1] The juvenile justice system was widely heralded as "one of the greatest advances in child welfare that has ever occurred" and "an integral part of total welfare planning."[2] Charles Chute, an enthusiastic supporter of the child-saving movement, claimed that "no single event has contributed more to the welfare of children and their families. It revolutionized the treatment of delinquent and neglected children and led to the passage of similar laws throughout the world."[3] Scholars from a variety of disciplines, such as the American sociologist George Herbert Mead and the German psychiatrist August Aichhorn, agreed that the juvenile court system represented a triumph of progressive liberalism over the forces of reaction and ignorance.[4]

[1]See, for example, The President's Commission on Law Enforcement and Administration of Justice, *Juvenile Delinquency and Youth Crime* (Washington D.C.: U.S. Government Printing Office, 1967), pp. 2–4.

[2]Charles L. Chute, "The Juvenile Court in Retrospect," 13 *Federal Probation* (September, 1949), p. 7; Harrison A. Dobbs, "In Defense of Juvenile Court," *Ibid.*, p. 29.

[3]Charles L. Chute, "Fifty Years of the Juvenile Court," *National Probation and Parole Association Yearbook* (1949), p. 1.

[4]George H. Mead, "The Psychology of Punitive Justice," 23 *American Journal of Sociology* (March, 1918), pp. 577–602; August Aichhorn, "The Juvenile Court; Is It a Solution?", in *Delinquency and Child Guidance: Selected Papers* (New York: International Universities Press, 1964), pp. 55–79.

More recently, the juvenile court and related reforms have been characterized as a "reflection of the humanitarianism that flowered in the last decades of the 19th century"[5] and an indication of "America's great sense of philanthropy and private concern about the common weal."[6]

Histories and accounts of the child-saving movement tend either to represent an "official" perspective or to imply a gradualist view of social progress.[7] This latter view is typified in Robert Pickett's study of the House of Refuge movement in New York in the middle of the last century:[8]

> In the earlier era, it had taken a band of largely religiously motivated humanitarians to see a need and move to meet that need. Although much of their vision eventually would be supplanted by more enlightened policies and techniques and far more elaborate support mechanisms, the main outlines of their program, which included mild discipline, academic and moral education, vocational training, the utilization of surrogate parents, and probationary surveillance, have stood the test of time. The survival of many of the notions of the founders of the House of Refuge testifies, at least in part, to their creative genius in meeting human needs. Their motivations may have been mixed and their oversights many, but

[5]Murray Levine and Adeline Levine, *A Social History of Helping Services: Clinic, Court, School, and Community* (New York: Appleton-Century-Crofts, 1970), p. 156.

[6]Gerhard O. W. Mueller, *History of American Criminal Law Scholarship* (New York: Walter E. Meyer Research Institute of Law, 1962), p. 113.

[7]See, for example, Herbert H. Lou, *Juvenile Courts in the United States* (Chapel Hill: University of North Carolina Press, 1927); Negley K. Teeters and John Otto Reinmann, *The Challenge of Delinquency* (Englewood Cliffs, N.J.: Prentice-Hall, 1950); and Ola Nyquist, *Juvenile Justice* (London: Macmillan, 1960).

[8]Robert S. Pickett, *House of Refuge: Origins of Juvenile Reform in New York State, 1815–1857* (Syracuse: Syracuse University Press, 1969), p. 188.

their efforts contributed to a considerable advance in the care and treatment of wayward youth.

This view of the 19th century reform movement as fundamentally benevolent, humanitarian, and gradualist is shared by most historians and criminologists who have written about the Progressive era. They argue that this reform impulse has its roots in the earliest ideals of modern liberalism and that it is part of a continuing struggle to overcome injustice and fulfill the promise of American life.[9] At the same time, these writers recognize that reform movements often degenerate into crusades and suffer from excessive idealism and moral absolutism.[10] The faults and limitations of the child-saving movement, for example, are generally explained in terms of the psychological tendency of its leaders to adopt attitudes of rigidity and moral righteousness. But this form of criticism is misleading because it overlooks larger political issues and depends too much on a subjective critique.

Although the Progressive era was a period of considerable change and reform in all areas of social, legal, political, and economic life, its history has been garnished with various myths. Conventional historical analysis, typified by the work of American historians in the 1940s and 1950s, promoted the view that American history consisted of regular confrontations between vested economic interests and various popular reform movements.[11] For Arthur Schlesinger, Jr., "liberalism in America has been ordinarily the movement of the other sections of society to restrain the power of the business community."[12] Simi-

[9]See, for example, Arthur M. Schlesinger, *The American as Reformer* (Cambridge: Harvard University Press, 1950).

[10]See, for example, Richard Hofstadter, *The Age of Reform* (New York: Vintage Books, 1955) and Joseph R. Gusfield, *Symbolic Crusade: Status Politics and the American Temperance Movement* (Urbana: University of Illinois Press, 1963).

[11]R. Jackson Wilson (Ed.) *Reform, Crisis, and Confusion, 1900–1929* (New York: Random House, 1970), especially pp. 3–6.

[12]Arthur M. Schlesinger, Jr., *The Age of Jackson* (Boston: Little, Brown, 1946), p. 505.

larly, Louis Hartz characterizes "liberal reform" as a "movement which emerged toward the end of the nineteenth century to adapt classical liberalism to the purposes of small propertied interests and the labor class and at the same time which rejected socialism."[13]

Conventional histories of progressivism argue that the reformers, who were for the most part drawn from the urban middle classes, were opposed to big business and felt victimized by the rapid changes in the economy, especially the emergence of the corporation as the dominant form of financial enterprise.[14] Their reform efforts were aimed at curbing the power of big business, eliminating corruption from the urban political machines, and extending the powers of the state through federal regulation of the economy and the development of a vision of "social responsibility" in local government. They were joined in this mission by sectors of the working class who shared their alienation and many of their grievances. For liberal historians like Richard Hofstadter, this alliance represented part of a continuing theme in American politics:[15]

> It has been the function of the liberal tradition in American politics, from the time of Jeffersonian democracy down through Populism, Progressivism, and the New Deal, at first to broaden the numbers of those who could benefit from the great American bonanza and then to humanize its workings and help heal its casualties. Without this sustained tradition of opposition and protest, and reform, the American system would not have been, as in times and places it was, nothing but a jungle, and would probably have failed to develop into the remarkable system for production and distribution that it is.

[13]Louis Hartz, *The Liberal Tradition in America* (New York: Harcourt, Brace & World, 1955), p. 228.
[14]Hofstadter, *op. cit.*, chapter IV.
[15]*Ibid.*, p. 18.

The political and racial crises of the 1960s, however, provoked a reevaluation of this earlier view of the liberal tradition in American politics, a tradition which appeared bankrupt in the face of rising crime rates, ghetto rebellions, and widespread protests against the state and its agencies of criminal justice. In the field of criminology, this reevaluation took place in national commissions such as the Kerner Commission and President Johnson's Commission on Law Enforcement and the Administration of Justice. Johnson's Crime Commission, as it is known, included a lengthy and detailed analysis of the juvenile justice system and its ineffectiveness in dealing with juvenile delinquency.

The Crime Commission's view of the juvenile justice system is cautious and pragmatic, designed to "shore up" institutional deficiencies and modernize the system's efficiency and accountability. Noting the rising rate of juvenile delinquency, increasing disrespect for constituted authority, and the failure of reformatories to rehabilitate offenders, the Commission attributes the failures of the juvenile justice system to the "grossly overoptimistic" expectations of 19th century reformers and the "community's continuing unwillingness to provide the resources— the people and facilities and concern—necessary to permit [the juvenile courts] to realize their potential...."[16] This view of the *unrealistic* quality of American liberalism was observed earlier by Richard Hofstadter:[17]

> My criticism ... is ... not that the Progressives most typically undermined or smashed standards, but that they set impossible standards, that they were victimized, in brief, by a form of moral absolutism.... A great part of both the strength and the weaknesses of our national existence lies in the fact that Americans

[16]The President's Commission on Law Enforcement and Administration of Justice, *op. cit.*, pp. 7, 8.

[17]Hofstadter, *op. cit.*, p. 16.

do not abide very quietly the evils of life. We are forever restlessly pitting ourselves against them, demanding changes, improvements, remedies, but not often with sufficient sense of the limits that the human condition will in the end insistently impose upon us.

Or as the Crime Commission stated it, "failure is most striking when hopes are highest."[18]

In this essay it will be argued that the above views and interpretations of juvenile justice are factually inaccurate and suffer from a serious misconception about the functions of modern liberalism.

PREVAILING MYTHS

The prevailing myths about the juvenile justice system can be summarized as follows: (1) The child-saving movement in the late 19th century was successful in humanizing the criminal justice system, rescuing children from jails and prisons, developing humanitarian judicial and penal institutions for juveniles, and defending the poor against economic and political exploitation. (2) The child-savers were "disinterested" reformers, representing an enlightened and socially responsible urban middle class, and opposed to big business. (3) The failures of the juvenile justice system are attributable partly to the overoptimism and moral absolutism of earlier reformers and partly to bureaucratic inefficiency and a lack of fiscal resources and trained personnel.

These myths are grounded in a liberal conception of American history that characterizes the child-savers as part of a much larger reform movement directed at restraining the power of political and business elites. In contrast, I will offer evidence that the child-saving movement

[18]The President's Commission on Law Enforcement and Administration of Justice, *op. cit.*, p. 7.

was a coercive and conservatizing influence, that liberalism in the Progressive era was the conscious product of policies initiated or supported by leaders of major corporations and financial institutions, and that many social reformers wanted to secure existing political and economic arrangements, albeit in an ameliorated and regulated form.

THE CHILD-SAVING MOVEMENT

Although the modern juvenile justice system can be traced in part to the development of various charitable and institutional programs in the early 19th century,[19] it was not until the close of the century that the modern system was systematically organized to include juvenile courts, probation, child guidance clinics, truant officers, and reformatories. The child-saving movement—an amalgam of philanthropists, middle-class reformers, and professionals—was responsible for the consolidation of these reforms.[20]

The 1890s represented for many middle-class intellectuals and professionals a period of discovery of "dim attics and damp cellars in poverty-stricken sections of populous towns" and "innumerable haunts of misery throughout the land."[21] The city was suddenly discovered to be a place of scarcity, disease, neglect, ignorance, and "dangerous influences." Its slums were the "last resorts of the

[19]For discussions of earlier reform movements, see Pickett, *loc. cit.* and Sanford J. Fox, "Juvenile Justice Reform: An Historical Perspective," 22 *Stanford Law Review* (June, 1970), pp. 1187–1239.

[20]The child-saving movement was broad and diverse, including reformers interested in child welfare, education, reformatories, labor and other related issues. This paper is limited primarily to child-savers involved in anti-delinquency reforms and should not be interpreted as characterizing the child-saving movement in general.

[21]William P. Letchworth, "Children of the State," National Conference of Charities and Correction, *Proceedings* (St. Paul, Minnesota, 1886), p. 138.

penniless and the criminal"; here humanity reached the lowest level of degradation and despair.[22] These conditions were not new to American urban life and the working class had been suffering such hardships for many years. Since the Haymarket Riot of 1886, the centers of industrial activity had been continually plagued by strikes, violent disruptions, and widespread business failures.

What distinguished the late 1890s from earlier periods was the recognition by some sectors of the privileged classes that far-reaching economic, political, and social reforms were desperately needed to restore order and stability. In the economy, these reforms were achieved through the corporation which extended its influence into all aspects of domestic and foreign policies so that by the 1940s some 139 corporations owned 45 percent of all the manufacturing assets in the country. It was the aim of corporate capitalists to limit traditional laissez-faire business competition and to transform the economy into a rational and interrelated system, characterized by extensive long-range planning and bureaucratic routine.[23] In politics, these reforms were achieved nationally by extending the regulatory powers of the federal government and locally by the development of commission and city manager forms of government as an antidote to corrupt machine politics. In social life, economic and political reforms were paralleled by the construction of new social service bureaucracies which regulated crime, education, health, labor, and welfare.

The child-saving movement tried to do for the criminal justice system what industrialists and corporate leaders were trying to do for the economy, that is, achieve order, stability, and control while preserving the existing class system and distribution of wealth. While the child-saving

[22]R. W. Hill, "The Children of Shinbone Alley," National Conference of Charities and Correction, *Proceedings* (Omaha, 1887), p. 231.
[23]William Appleman Williams, *The Contours of American History* (Chicago: Quadrangle Books, 1966), especially pp. 345–412.

movement, like most Progressive reforms, drew its most active and visible supporters from the middle-class and professions, it would not have been capable of achieving significant reforms without the financial and political support of the wealthy and powerful. Such support was not without precedent in various philanthropic movements preceding the child-savers. New York's Society for the Reformation of Juvenile Delinquents benefited in the 1820s from the contributions of Stephen Allen, whose many influential positions included Mayor of New York and president of the New York Life Insurance and Trust Company.[24] The first large gift to the New York Children's Aid Society, founded in 1853, was donated by Mrs. William Astor.[25] According to Charles Loring Brace, who helped to found the Children's Aid Society, "a very superior class of young men consented to serve on our Board of Trustees; men who, in their high principles of duty, and in the obligations which they feel are imposed by wealth and position, bid fair hereafter to make the name of New York merchants respected as it was never before throughout the country."[26] Elsewhere, welfare charities similarly benefited from the donations and bequests of the upper class.[27] Girard College, one of the first large orphanages in the United States, was built and furnished with funds from the banking fortune of Stephen Girard;[28] and the Catholic bankers and financiers of New York helped to mobilize support and money for various Catholic charities.[29]

[24]Pickett, op. cit., pp. 50–55.
[25]Committee on the History of Child-Saving Work, History of Child-Saving in the United States (National Conference of Charities and Correction, 1893), p. 5.
[26]Charles Loring Brace, The Dangerous Classes of New York and Twenty Years' Work Among Them (New York: Wynkoop and Hallenbeck, 1880), pp. 282–83.
[27]Committee on the History of Child-Saving Work, op. cit., pp. 70–73.
[28]Ibid., pp. 80–81.
[29]Ibid., p. 270.

The child-saving movement similarly enjoyed the support of propertied and powerful individuals. In Chicago, for example, where the movement had some of its most notable successes, the child-savers included Louise Bowen and Ellen Henrotin who were both married to bankers;[30] Mrs. Potter Palmer, whose husband owned vast amounts of land and property, was an ardent child-saver when not involved in the exclusive Fortnightly Club, the elite Chicago Woman's Club or the Board of Lady Managers of the World's Fair;[31] another child-saver in Chicago, Mrs. Perry Smith, was married to the vice-president of the Chicago and Northwestern Railroad. Even the more radically-minded child-savers came from upper-class backgrounds. The fathers of Jane Addams and Julia Lathrop, for example, were both lawyers and Republican senators in the Illinois legislature. Jane Addams' father was one of the richest men in northern Illinois, and her stepbrother, Harry Haldeman, was a socialite from Baltimore who later amassed a large fortune in Kansas City.[32]

The child-saving movement was not simply a humanistic enterprise on behalf of the lower classes against the established order. On the contrary, its impetus came primarily from the middle and upper classes who were instrumental in devising new forms of social control to protect their privileged positions in American society. The child-saving movement was not an isolated phenomenon but rather reflected massive changes in economic relationships, from laissez-faire to monopoly capitalism, and in strategies of social control, from inefficient repres-

[30]For more about these child-savers, see Anthony Platt, *The Child-Savers: The Invention of Delinquency* (Chicago: University of Chicago Press, 1969), pp. 75–100.

[31]Louise C. Wade, *Graham Taylor: Pioneer for Social Justice, 1851–1938* (Chicago: University of Chicago Press, 1964), p. 59.

[32]G. William Domhoff, *The Higher Circles: The Governing Class in America* (New York: Random House, 1970), p. 48 and Platt, *op. cit.*, pp. 92–98.

sion to welfare state benevolence.[33] This reconstruction of economic and social institutions, which was not achieved without conflict within the ruling class, represented a victory for the more "enlightened" wing of corporate liberal reforms.[34]

Many large corporations and business leaders, for example, supported federal regulation of the economy in order to protect their own investments and stabilize the marketplace. Business leaders and political spokesmen were often in basic agreement about fundamental economic issues. "There was no conspiracy during the Progressive Era," notes Gabriel Kolko. "There was basic agreement among political and business leaders as to what was the public good, and no one had to be cajoled in a sinister manner."[35] In his analysis of liberal ideology in the Progressive era, James Weinstein similarly argues that "few reforms were enacted without the tacit approval, if not the guidance, of the large corporate interests." For the corporation executives, liberalism meant "the responsibility of all classes to maintain and increase the efficiency of the existing social order."[36]

[33]"The transformation in penal systems cannot be explained only from changing needs of the war against crime, although this struggle does play a part. Every system of production tends to discover punishments which correspond to its productive relationships. It is thus necessary to investigate the origin and fate of penal systems, the use or avoidance of specific punishments, and the intensity of penal practices as they are determined by social forces, above all by economic and then fiscal forces." Georg Rusche and Otto Kirchheimer, *Punishment and Social Structure* (New York: Russell & Russell, 1968), p. 5.

[34]See, for example, Gabriel Kolko, *The Triumph of Conservatism: A Reinterpretation of American History, 1900–1916* (Chicago: Quadrangle Books, 1967); James Weinstein, *The Corporate Ideal in the Liberal State, 1900–1918* (Boston: Beacon Press, 1969); Samuel Haber, *Efficiency and Uplift: Scientific Management in the Progressive Era, 1890–1920* (Chicago: University of Chicago Press, 1964); and Robert H. Wiebe, *Businessmen and Reform: A Study of the Progressive Movement* (Cambridge: Harvard University Press, 1962).

[35]Kolko, *op. cit.*, p. 282.

[36]Weinstein, *op. cit.*, pp. ix, xi.

Progressivism was in part a businessmen's movement and big business played a central role in the Progressive coalition's support of welfare reforms. Child labor legislation in New York, for example, was supported by several groups, including upper-class industrialists who did not depend on cheap child labor. According to Jeremy Felt's history of that movement, "the abolition of child labor could be viewed as a means of driving out marginal manufacturers and tenement operators, hence increasing the consolidation and efficiency of business."[37] The rise of compulsory education, another welfare state reform, was also closely tied to the changing forms of industrial production and social control. Charles Loring Brace, writing in the mid-nineteenth century, anticipated the use of education as preparation for industrial discipline when, "in the interests of public order, of liberty, of property, for the sake of our own safety and the endurance of free institutions here," he advocated "a strict and careful law, which shall compel every minor to learn and read and write, under severe penalties in case of disobedience."[38] By the end of the century, the working class had imposed upon them a sterile and authoritarian educational system which mirrored the ethos of the corporate workplace and was designed to provide "an increasingly refined training and selection mechanism for the labor force."[39]

While the child-saving movement was supported and financed by corporate liberals, the day-to-day work of lobbying, public education and organizing was undertaken by middle-class urban reformers, professionals and special

[37]Jeremy P. Felt, *Hostages of Fortune: Child Labor Reform in New York State* (Syracuse: Syracuse University Press, 1965), p. 45.

[38]Brace, *op. cit.*, p. 352.

[39]David K. Cohen and Marvin Lazerson, "Education and the Corporate Order," 8 *Socialist Revolution* (March–April, 1972), p. 50. See, also Michael B. Katz, *The Irony of Early School Reform: Educational Innovation in Mid-Nineteenth Century Massachusetts* (Cambridge: Harvard University Press, 1968), and Lawrence A. Cremin, *The Transformation of the School: Progressivism in American Education, 1876–1957* (New York: Vintage, 1961).

interest groups. The more moderate and conservative sectors of the feminist movement were especially active in anti-delinquency reforms.[40] Their successful participation derived in part from public stereotypes of women as the "natural caretakers" of "wayward children." Women's claim to the public care of children had precedent during the nineteenth century and their role in child rearing was paramount. Women, generally regarded as better teachers than men, were more influential in child training and discipline at home. The fact that public education also came more under the direction of women teachers in the schools served to legitimize the predominance of women in other areas of "child saving."[41]

The child-saving movement attracted women from a variety of political and class backgrounds, though it was dominated by the daughters of the old landed gentry and wives of the upper-class nouveau riche. Career women and society philanthropists, elite women's clubs and settlement houses, and political and civic organizations worked together on the problems of child care, education, and juvenile delinquency. Professional and political women's groups regarded child-saving as a problem of women's rights, whereas their opponents seized upon it as an opportunity to keep women in their "proper place."

[40]It should be emphasized that child-saving reforms were predominantly supported by more privileged sectors of the feminist movement, especially those who had an interest in developing professional careers in education, social work and probation. In recent years, radical feminists have emphasized that "we must include the oppression of children in any program for feminist revolution or we will be subject to the same failing of which we have so often accused men: of not having gone deep enough in our analysis, of having missed an important substratum of oppression merely because it didn't directly concern *us*." Shulamith Firestone, *The Dialectic of Sex: The Case for Feminist Revolution* (New York: Bantam, 1971), p. 104.

[41]Robert Sunley, "Early Nineteenth Century American Literature on Child-Rearing," in Margaret Mead and Martha Wolfenstein (Eds.), *Childhood in Contemporary Cultures* (Chicago: University of Chicago Press, 1955), p. 152; see, also, Orville G. Brim, *Education for Child-Rearing* (New York: Free Press, 1965), pp. 321–49.

Child-saving became a reputable task for any woman who wanted to extend her "housekeeping" functions into the community without denying antifeminist stereotypes of woman's nature and place.[42]

For traditionally educated women and daughters of the landed and industrial gentry, the child-saving movement presented an opportunity for pursuing socially acceptable public roles and for restoring some of the authority and spiritual influence that many women felt they had lost through the urbanization of family life. Their traditional functions were dramatically threatened by the weakening of domestic roles and the specialized rearrangement of the family.[43] The child savers were aware that their championship of social outsiders such as immigrants, the poor, and children, was not wholly motivated by disinterested ideals of justice and equality. Philanthropic work filled a void in their own lives, a void that was created in part by the decline of traditional religion, increased leisure and boredom, the rise of public education, and the breakdown of communal life in large, crowded cities. "By simplifying dress and amusements, by cutting off a little here and there from our luxuries," wrote one child-saver, "we may change the whole current of many human lives."[44] Women were exhorted to make their lives useful by participating in welfare programs, by volunteering their time and services, and by getting acquainted with less privileged groups. They were also encouraged to seek work in institutions that were "like family-life with its many-sided development and varied interests and occu-

[42]For an extended discussion of this issue, see Platt, *loc. cit.* and Christopher Lasch, *The New Radicalism in America, 1889–1963: The Intellectual as a Social Type* (New York: Alfred A. Knopf, 1965), pp. 3–68.

[43]Talcott Parsons and Robert F. Bales, *Family, Socialization and Interaction Process* (Glencoe, Illinois: Free Press, 1955), pp. 3–33.

[44]Clara T. Leonard, "Family Homes for Pauper and Dependent Children," Annual Conference of Charities, *Proceedings* (Chicago, 1879), p. 175.

pations, and where the woman-element shall pervade the house and soften its social atmosphere with motherly tenderness."[45]

While the child-saving movement can be partly understood as a "symbolic crusade"[46] which served ceremonial and status functions for many women, it was by no means a reactionary and romantic movement, nor was it supported only by women and members of the old gentry. Child-saving also had considerable instrumental significance for legitimizing new career openings for women. The new role of social worker combined elements of an old and partly fictitious role (defender of family life) and elements of a new role: social servant. Social work and professional child saving provided new opportunities for career-minded women who found the traditional professions dominated and controlled by men.[47] These child savers were members of the emerging bourgeoisie created by the new industrial order.

It is not surprising that the professions also supported the child-saving movement, for they were capable of reaping enormous economic and status rewards from the changes taking place. The clergy had nothing to lose (but more of their rapidly declining constituency) and everything to gain by incorporating social services into traditional religion. Lawyers were needed for their technical expertise and to administer new institutions. And academics discovered a new market which paid them as consultants, elevated them to positions of national prestige, and furnished endless materials for books, articles, and conferences. As Richard Hofstadter has noted:[48]

[45]W. P. Lynde, "Prevention in Some of its Aspects," *Ibid.*, pp. 165–166.

[46]Joseph R. Gusfield, *Symbolic Crusade, loc. cit.*

[47]See, generally, Roy Lubove, *The Professional Altruist: The Emergence of Social Work as a Career, 1880–1930* (Cambridge: Harvard University Press, 1965).

[48]Hofstadter, *op. cit.*, p. 155.

The development of regulative and human legislation required the skills of lawyers and economists,
sociologists and political scientists, in the writing of
laws and in the staffing of administrative and regulative bodies. Controversy over such issues created a
new market for the books and magazine articles of
the experts and engendered a new respect for their
specialized knowledge. Reform brought with it the
brain trust.

While the rank and file reformers in the child-saving
movement worked closely with corporate liberals, it
would be inaccurate to simply characterize them as lack-
eys of big business. Many were principled and genuinely
concerned about alleviating human misery and improving the lives of the poor. Moreover, many women who
participated in the movement were able to free themselves from male domination and participate more fully in
society. But for the most part, the child savers and other
Progressive reformers defended capitalism and rejected
socialist alternatives. Most reformers accepted the structure of the new industrial order and sought to moderate
its cruder inequities and reduce inharmonies in the existing system.[49] Though many child savers were "socialists of
the heart" and ardent critics of society, their programs
were typically reformist and did not alter basic economic
inequalities.[50] Rhetoric and righteous indignation were
more prevalent than programs of action to modify the
antecedent conditions of social injustice.

The intellectual and professional communities did little
to criticize Progressive reforms, partly because so many
benefited from their new role as government consultants
and experts, and partly because their conception of social
change was limited and elitist. As Jackson Wilson observed, many intellectuals in the Progressive movement

[49]Williams, *op. cit.*, p. 373 and Weinstein, *op. cit.*, p. 254.
[50]Williams, *op. cit.*, pp. 374, 395–402.

were "interested in creating a system of government which would allow the people to rule only at a carefully kept distance and at infrequent intervals, reserving most real power and planning to a corps of experts and professionals."[51] Those few reformers who had a genuine concern for liberating the lives of the poor by considering socialist alternatives were either co-opted by their allies, betrayed by their own class interests, or became the prisoners of social and economic forces beyond their control.[52]

IMAGES OF CRIME AND DELINQUENCY

The child-saving reformers were part of a much larger movement to readjust institutions to conform to the requirements of corporate capitalism and the modern welfare state. As the country emerged from the depressions and industrial violence of the late 19th century, efforts were made to rescue and regulate capitalism through developing a new political economy, designed to stabilize production and profits. The stability and smooth functioning of this new order depended heavily on the capacity of welfare state institutions, especially the schools, to achieve cultural hegemony and guarantee loyalty to the state. As William Appleman Williams has commented, "it is almost impossible to overemphasize the importance of the very general—yet dynamic and powerful—concept that the country faced a fateful choice between order and chaos."[53] In order to develop support for and legitimize the corporate liberal state, a new ideology was promoted in which chaos was equated with crime and violence, and

[51]R. Jackson Wilson, "United States: the Reassessment of Liberalism," *Journal of Contemporary History* (January, 1967), p. 96.
[52]Ralph Miliband, *The State in Capitalist Society* (New York: Basic Books, 1969), pp. 265–277.
[53]Williams, *op. cit.*, p. 356.

salvation was to be found in the development of new and more extensive forms of social control.

The child savers viewed the "criminal classes" with a mixture of contempt and benevolence. Crime was portrayed as rising from the "lowest orders" and threatening to engulf "respectable" society like a virulent disease. Charles Loring Brace, a leading child-saver, typified popular and professional views about crime and delinquency:

> As Christian men, we cannot look upon this great multitude of unhappy, deserted, and degraded boys and girls without feeling our responsibility to God for them. The class increases: immigration is pouring in its multitudes of poor foreigners who leave these young outcasts everywhere in our midst. These boys and girls ... will soon form the great lower class of our city. They will influence elections; they may shape the policy of the city; they will assuredly, if unreclaimed, poison society all around them. They will help to form the great multitude of robbers, thieves, and vagrants, who are now such a burden upon the law-respecting community. . . .[54]

This attitude of contempt derived from a view of criminals as less-than-human, a perspective that was strongly influenced and aggravated by nativist and racist ideologies.[55] The "criminal class" was variously described as "creatures" living in "burrows," "dens," and "slime"; as "little Arabs" and "foreign childhood that floats along the streets and docks of the city—vagabondish, thievish, familiar with the vicious ways and places of the town";[56] and as "ignorant," "shiftless," "indolent," and "dissipated."[57]

[54]Committee on the History of Child-Saving Work, *op. cit.*, p. 3.

[55]See, generally, John Higham, *Strangers in the Land: Patterns of American Nativism, 1860–1925* (New York: Atheneum, 1965).

[56]Brace, *op. cit.*, pp. 30, 49; Bradford Kinney Peirce, *A Half Century with Juvenile Delinquents* (Montclair, New Jersey: Patterson Smith, 1969, originally published 1869), p. 253.

[57]Nathan Allen, "Prevention of Crime and Pauperism," Annual Conference of Charities, *Proceedings* (Cincinnati, 1878), pp. 111–24.

The child-savers were alarmed and frightened by the "dangerous classes" whose "very number makes one stand aghast," noted the urban reformer Jacob Riis.[58] Law and order were widely demanded:[59]

> The "dangerous classes" of New York are mainly American-born, but the children of Irish and German immigrants. They are as ignorant as London flashmen or costermongers. They are far more brutal than the peasantry from whom they descend, and they are much banded together, in associations, such as "Dead Rabbit," "Plug-ugly," and various target companies. They are our *enfant perdus,* grown up to young manhood. . . . They are ready for any offense or crime, however degraded or bloody. . . . Let but Law lift its hand from them for a season, or let the civilizing influences of American life fail to reach them, and, if the opportunity offered, we should see an explosion from this class which might leave this city in ashes and blood.

These views derived considerable legitimacy from prevailing theories of social and reform Darwinism which, *inter alia,* proposed that criminals were a dangerous and atavistic class, standing outside the boundaries of morally regulated relationships. Herbert Spencer's writings had a major impact on American intellectuals and Cesare Lombroso, perhaps the most significant figure in 19th century criminology, looked for recognition in the United States when he felt that his experiments on the "criminal type" had been neglected in Europe.[60]

Although Lombroso's theoretical and experimental studies were not translated into English until 1911, his

[58]Jacob A. Riis, *How the Other Half Lives* (New York: Hill and Wang, 1957, originally published in 1890), p. 134.

[59]Brace, *op. cit.*, pp. 27, 29.

[60]See, for example, Lombroso's comments in the Introduction to Arthur MacDonald, *Criminology* (New York: Funk and Wagnalls, 1893).

findings were known by American academics in the early 1890s, and their popularity, like that of Spencer's works, was based on the fact that they confirmed widely-held stereotypes about the biological basis and inferior character of a "criminal class." A typical view was expressed by Nathan Allen in 1878 at the National Conference of Charities and Correction: "If our object is to prevent crime in a large scale, we must direct attention to its main sources—to the materials that make criminals; the springs must be dried up; the supplies must be cut off."[61] This was to be achieved, if necessary, by birth control and eugenics. Similar views were expressed by Hamilton Wey, an influential physician at Elmira Reformatory, who argued before the National Prison Association in 1881 that criminals had to be treated as a "distinct type of human species."[62]

Literature on "social degradation" was extremely popular during the 1870s and 1880s, though most such "studies" were little more than crude and racist polemics, padded with moralistic epithets and preconceived value judgments. Richard Dugdale's series of papers on the Jukes family, which became a model for the case-study approach to social problems, was distorted almost beyond recognition by antiintellectual supporters of hereditary theories of crime.[63] Confronted by the evidence of Darwin, Galton, Dugdale, Caldwell, and many other disciples of the biological image of behavior, many child savers were compelled to admit that "a large proportion of the unfortunate children that go to make up the great army

[61]Allen, loc. cit.

[62]Hamilton D. Wey, "A Plea for Physical Training of Youthful Criminals," National Prison Association, Proceedings (Boston: 1888), pp. 181–93. For further discussion of this issue, see Platt, op. cit., pp. 18–28 and Arthur E. Fink, Causes of Crime: Biological Theories in the United States, 1800–1915 (New York: A. S. Barnes, 1962).

[63]Richard L. Dugdale, The Jukes: A Study in Crime, Pauperism, Disease, and Heredity (New York: G. P. Putnam's Sons, 1877).

of criminals are not born right."[64] Reformers adopted and modified the rhetoric of social Darwinism in order to emphasize the urgent need for confronting the "crime problem" before it got completely out of hand. A popular proposal, for example, was the "methodized registration and training" of potential criminals, "or these failing, their early and entire withdrawal from the community."[65]

Although some child savers advocated drastic methods of crime control, including birth control through sterilization, cruel punishments, and life-long incarceration, more moderate views prevailed. This victory for moderation was related to the recognition by many Progressive reformers that short-range repression was counterproductive as well as cruel and that long-range planning and amelioration were required to achieve economic and political stability. The rise of more benevolent strategies of social control occurred at about the same time that influential capitalists were realizing that existing economic arrangements could not be successfully maintained unless private police and government troops were made available to them.[66] While the child savers justified their reforms as humanitarian, it is clear that this humanitarianism reflected their class background and elitist conceptions of human potentiality. The child-savers shared the view of more conservative professionals that "criminals" were a distinct and dangerous class, indigenous to working-class culture, and a threat to "civilized" society. They differed mainly in the procedures by which the "criminal class" should be controlled or neutralized.

Gradually, a more "enlightened" view about strategies

[64]Sarah B. Cooper, "The Kindergarten as Child-Saving Work." National Conference of Charities and Correction, *Proceedings* (Madison, 1883), pp. 130–38.

[65]I. N. Kerlin, "The Moral Imbecile," National Conference of Charities and Correction, *Proceedings* (Baltimore, 1890), pp. 244–50.

[66]Williams, *op. cit.*, p. 354.

of control prevailed among the leading representatives of professional associations. Correctional workers, for example, did not want to think of themselves merely as the custodians of a pariah class. The self-image of penal reformers as "doctors" rather than "guards," and the medical domination of criminological research in the United States at that time facilitated the acceptance of "therapeutic" strategies in prisons and reformatories.[67] Physicians gradually provided the official rhetoric of penal reform, replacing cruder concepts of social Darwinism with a new optimism. Admittedly, the criminal was "pathological" and "diseased," but medical science offered the possibility of miraculous cures. Although there was a popular belief in the existence of a "criminal class" separated from the rest of humanity by a "vague boundary line," there was no good reason why this class could not be identified, diagnosed, segregated, changed, and incorporated back into society.[68]

By the late 1890s, most child savers agreed that hereditary theories of crime were overfatalistic. The superintendant of the Kentucky Industrial School of Reform, for example, told delegates to a national conference on corrections that heredity is "unjustifiably made a bugaboo to discourage efforts at rescue. We know that physical heredity tendencies can be neutralized and often nullified by proper counteracting precautions."[69] E. R. L. Gould, a sociologist at the University of Chicago, similarly criticized biological theories of crime as unconvincing and sentimental. "Is it not better," he said, "to postulate free-

[67]Fink, op. cit., p. 247.
[68]See, for example, Illinois Board of State Commissioners of Public Charities, *Second Biennial Report* (Springfield: State Journal Steam Print, 1873), pp. 195–96.
[69]Peter Caldwell, "The Duty of the State to Delinquent Children," National Conference of Charities and Correction, *Proceedings* (New York, 1898), pp. 404–10.

dom of choice than to preach the doctrine of the unfettered will, and so elevate criminality into a propitiary sacrifice?"[70]

Charles Cooley, writing in 1896, was one of the first American sociologists to observe that criminal behavior depended as much upon social and economic circumstances as it did upon the inheritance of biological traits. "The criminal class," he observed, "is largely the result of society's bad workmanship upon fairly good material." In support of this argument, he noted that there was a "large and fairly trustworthy body of evidence" to suggest that many "degenerates" could be converted into "useful citizens by rational treatment."[71]

Although there was a wide difference of opinion among experts as to the precipitating causes of crime, it was generally agreed that criminals were abnormally conditioned by a multitude of biological and environmental forces, some of which were permanent and irreversible. Strictly biological theories of crime were modified to incorporate a developmental view of human behavior. If, as it was believed, criminals are conditioned by biological heritage and brutish living conditions, then prophylactic measures must be taken early in life. "We must get hold of the little waifs that grow up to form the criminal element just as early in life as possible," exhorted an influential child saver. "Hunt up the children of poverty, of crime, and of brutality, just as soon as they can be reached."[72] Efforts were needed to reach the criminals of future generations. "They are born to crime," wrote the

[70]E. R. L. Gould, "The Statistical Study of Hereditary Criminality," National Conference of Charities and Correction, *Proceedings* (New Haven, 1895), pp. 134–43.

[71]Charles H. Cooley, " 'Nature' v. 'Nurture' in the Making of Social Careers," National Conference of Charities and Correction, *Proceedings* (Grand Rapids, 1896), pp. 399–405.

[72]Committee on the History of Child-Saving Work, *op. cit.*, p. 90.

penologist Enoch Wines, "brought up for it. They must be saved."[73] New institutions and new programs were required to meet this challenge.

JUVENILE COURT

The essential preoccupation of the child-saving movement was the recognition and control of youthful deviance. It brought attention to, and thus "invented" new categories of youthful misbehavior that had been hitherto unappreciated. The efforts of the child-savers were institutionally expressed in the juvenile court which, despite recent legislative and constitutional reforms, is generally acknowledged as their most significant contribution to progressive penology. There is some dispute about which state first created a special tribunal for children. Massachusetts and New York passed laws, in 1874 and 1892 respectively, providing for the trials of minors apart from adults charged with crimes. Ben Lindsey, a renowned judge and reformer, also claimed this distinction for Colorado where a juvenile court was, in effect, established through an educational law of 1899. However, most authorities agree that the Juvenile Court Act, passed by the Illinois legislature in the same year, was the first official enactment to be recognized as a model statute by other states and countries.[74] By 1917, juvenile court legislation had been passed in all but three states and by 1932 there were over 600 independent juvenile courts throughout the United States.[75]

[73]Enoch C. Wines, *The State of Prisons and of Child-Saving Institutions in the Civilized World* (Cambridge: Harvard University Press, 1880).

[74]Helen Page Bates, "Digest of Statutes Relating to Juvenile Courts and Probation Systems," 13 *Charities* (January, 1905), pp. 329–36.

[75]Joel F. Handler, "The Juvenile Court and the Adversary System: Problems of Function and Form," 1965 *Wisconsin Law Review* (1965), pp. 7–51.

The juvenile court system was part of a general movement directed towards developing a specialized labor market and industrial discipline under corporate capitalism by creating new programs of adjudication and control for "delinquent," "dependent" and "neglected" youth. This in turn was related to augmenting the family and enforcing compulsory education in order to guarantee the proper reproduction of the labor force. For example, underlying the juvenile court system was the concept of *parens patriae* by which the courts were authorized to handle with wide discretion the problems of "its least fortunate junior citizens." The administration of juvenile justice, which differed in many important respects from the criminal court system, was delegated extensive powers of control over youth. A child was not accused of a crime but offered assistance and guidance; intervention in the lives of "delinquents" was not supposed to carry the stigma of criminal guilt. Judicial records were not generally available to the press or public, and juvenile hearings were typically conducted in private. Court procedures were informal and inquisitorial, not requiring the presence of a defense attorney. Specific criminal safeguards of due process were not applicable because juvenile proceedings were defined by statute as civil in character.[76]

The judges of the new court were empowered to investigate the character and social background of "predelinquent" as well as delinquent children; they concerned themselves with motivation rather than intent, seeking to identify the moral reputation of problematic children. The requirements of preventive penology and child saving further justified the court's intervention in cases where no offense has actually been committed, but where, for example, a child was posing problems for some

[76]Gustav L. Schramm, "The Juvenile Court Idea," 13 *Federal Probation* (September, 1949), p. 21.

person in authority, such as a parent or teacher or social worker.[77]

The role model for juvenile court judges was doctor-counselor rather than lawyer. "Judicial therapists" were expected to establish a one-to-one relationship with "delinquents" in the same way that a country doctor might give his time and attention to a favorite patient. Juvenile courtrooms were often arranged like a clinic and the vocabulary of its participants was largely composed of medical metaphors. "We do not know the child without a thorough examination," wrote Judge Julian Mack. "We must reach into the soul-life of the child."[78] Another judge from Los Angeles suggested that the juvenile court should be a "laboratory of human behavior" and its judges trained as "specialists in the art of human relations." It was the judge's task to "get the whole truth about a child" in the same way that a "physician searches for every detail that bears on the condition of the patient."[79] Similarly, the judges of the Boston juvenile court liked to think of themselves as "physicians in a dispensary."[80]

The unique character of the child-saving movement was its concerns for predelinquent offenders ("children who occupy the debatable ground between criminality and innocence"), and its claim that it could transform potential criminals into respectable citizens by training them in "habits of industry, self-control and obedience to law."[81] This policy justified the diminishing of traditional procedures and allowed police, judges, probation officers,

[77]Monrad G. Paulsen, "Fairness to the Juvenile Offender," 41 *Minnesota Law Review* (1957), pp. 547–67.

[78]Julian W. Mack, "The Chancery Procedure in the Juvenile Court," in Jane Addams (Ed.), *The Child, the Clinic and the Court* (New York: New Republic, 1925), p. 315.

[79]Miriam Van Waters, "The Socialization of Juvenile Court Procedure," 21 *Journal of Criminal Law and Criminology* (1922), pp. 61, 69.

[80]Harvey H. Baker, "Procedure of the Boston Juvenile Court," 23 *Survey* (February, 1910), p. 646.

[81]Illinois Board of State Commissioners of Public Charities, *Sixth Biennial Report* (Springfield: H. W. Rokker, 1880), p. 104.

and truant officers to work together without legal hindrance. If children were to be rescued, it was important that the rescuers be free to pursue their mission without the interference of defense lawyers and due process. Delinquents had to be saved, transformed, and reconstituted. "There is no essential difference," noted a prominent child saver, "between a criminal and any other sinner. The means and methods of restoration are the same for both."[82]

The juvenile court legislation enabled the state to investigate and control a wide variety of behaviors. As Joel Handler has observed, "the critical philosophical position of the reform movement was that no formal, legal distinctions should be made between the delinquent and the dependent or neglected."[83] Statutory definitions of "delinquency" encompassed (1) acts that would be criminal if committed by adults; (2) acts that violated county, town, or municipal ordinances; and (3) violations of vaguely worded catch-alls, such as "vicious or immoral behavior," "incorrigibility," and "truancy," which "seem to express the notion that the adolescent, if allowed to continue, will engage in more serious conduct."[84]

The juvenile court movement went far beyond a concern for special treatment of adolescent offenders. It brought within the ambit of governmental control a set of youthful activities that had been previously ignored or dealt with on an informal basis. It was not by accident that the behavior subject to penalties—drinking, sexual "license," roaming the streets, begging, frequenting dance halls and movies, fighting, and being seen in public late at night—was especially characteristic of the children of

[82]Frederick H. Wines, "Reformation as an End in Prison Discipline," National Conference of Charities and Correction, *Proceedings* (Buffalo, 1888), p. 198.

[83]Joel F. Handler, *op. cit.*, p. 9.

[84]Joel F. Handler and Margaret K. Rosenheim, "Privacy and Welfare: Public Assistance and Juvenile Justice," 31 *Law and Contemporary Problems* (1966), pp. 377–412.

working-class and immigrant families. Once arrested and adjudicated, these "delinquents" became wards of the court and eligible for salvation.

REFORMATORY SYSTEM

It was through the reformatory system that the child savers hoped to demonstrate that delinquents were capable of being converted into law-abiding citizens. The reformatory was distinguished from the traditional penitentiary in several ways: it adopted a policy of indeterminate sentencing; it emphasized the importance of a countryside location; and it typically was organized on the "cottage" plan as opposed to the traditional congregate housing found in penitentiaries. The ultimate aim of the reformatory was reformation of the criminal, which could only be achieved "by placing the prisoner's fate, as far as possible, in his own hand, by enabling him, through industry and good conduct to raise himself, step by step, to a position of less restraint. . . ."[85]

Based on a crude theory of rewards and punishments, the "new penology" set itself the task of resocializing the "dangerous classes." The typical resident of a reformatory, according to one child saver, had been "cradled in infamy, imbibing with its earliest natural nourishment the germs of a depraved appetite, and reared in the midst of people whose lives are an atrocious crime against natural and divine law and the rights of society." In order to correct and reform such a person, the reformatory plan was designed to teach the value of adjustment, private enterprise, thrift, and self-reliance: "To make a good boy out of this bundle of perversities, his entire being must be revolutionized. He must be taught self-control, industry,

[85]From a report by Enoch Wines and Theodore Dwight to the New York legislature in 1867, quoted by Max Grünhut, *Penal Reform* (Oxford: Clarendon Press, 1948), p. 90.

respect for himself and the rights of others."[86] The real test of reformation in a delinquent, as William Letchworth told the National Conference of Charities and Correction in 1886, was his uncomplaining adjustment to his former environment. "If he is truly reformed in the midst of adverse influences," said Letchworth, "he gains that moral strength which makes his reform permanent."[87] Moreover, reformed delinquents were given every opportunity to rise "far above the class from which they sprang," especially if they were "patient" and "self-denying."[88]

Reformation of delinquents was to be achieved in a number of different ways. The trend from congregate housing to group living represented a significant change in the organization of penal institutions. The "cottage" plan was designed to provide more intensive supervision and to reproduce, symbolically at least, an atmosphere of family life conducive to the resocialization of youth. The "new penology" also urged the benefits of a rural location, partly in order to teach agricultural skills, but mainly in order to guarantee a totally controlled environment. This was justified by appealing to the romantic theory that corrupt delinquents would be spiritually regenerated by their contact with unspoiled nature.[89]

Education was stressed as the main form of industrial and moral training in reformatories. According to Michael Katz, in his study on 19th century education, the reformatory provided "the first form of compulsory schooling in the United States."[90] The prominence of education as a technique of reform reflected the widespread emphasis on socialization and assimilation instead of

[86]Peter Caldwell, "The Reform School Problem," National Conference of Charities and Correction, *Proceedings* (St. Paul, 1886), pp. 71–76.
[87]Letchworth, *op. cit.,* p. 152.
[88]Committee on the History of Child-Saving Work, *op. cit.,* p. 20.
[89]See Platt, *op. cit.,* pp. 55–66.
[90]Katz, *op. cit.,* p. 187.

cruder methods of social control. But as Georg Rusche and Otto Kirchheimer observed in their study of the relationship between economic and penal policies, the rise of "rehabilitative" and educational programs was "largely the result of opposition on the part of free workers," for "wherever working-class organizations were powerful enough to influence state politics, they succeeded in obtaining complete abolition of all forms of prison labor (Pennsylvania in 1897, for example), causing much suffering to the prisoners, or at least in obtaining very considerable limitations, such as work without modern machinery, conventional rather than modern types of prison industry, or work for the government instead of for the free market."[91]

Although the reformatory system, as envisioned by urban reformers, suffered in practice from overcrowding, mismanagement, inadequate financing, and staff hiring problems, its basic ideology was still tough-minded and uncompromising. As the American Friends Service Committee noted, "if the reformers were naive, the managers of the correctional establishment were not. Under the leadership of Zebulon R. Brockway of the Elmira Reformatory, by the latter part of the 19th century they had co-opted the reformers and consolidated their leadership and control of indeterminate sentence reform."[92] The child-savers were not averse to using corporal punishment and other severe disciplinary measures when inmates were recalcitrant. Brockway, for example, regarded his task as "socialization of the anti-social by scientific training while under complete governmental control."[93] To achieve this goal, Brockway's reformatory became "like a garrison of a thousand prisoner soldiers" and "every incipient disintegration was promptly checked and disinclination of individual prisoners to con-

[91]Rusche and Kirchheimer, *op. cit.*, pp. 131–132.
[92]American Friends Service Committee, *op. cit.*, p. 28.
[93]Zebulon R. Brockway, *Fifty Years of Prison Service* (New York: Charities Publication Committee, 1912), p. 393.

form was overcome."[94] Child-saving was a job for resolute professionals who realized that "sickly sentimentalism" had no place in their work.[95]

"Criminals shall either be cured," Brockway told the National Prison Congress in 1870, "or kept under such continued restraint as gives guarantee of safety from further depredations."[96] Restraint and discipline were an integral part of the "treatment" program and not merely expediencies of administration. Military drill, "training of the will," and long hours of tedious labor were the essence of the reformatory system and the indeterminate sentence policy guaranteed its smooth operation. "Nothing can tend more certainly to secure the most hardened and desperate criminals than the present system of short sentences," wrote the reformer Bradford Kinney Peirce in 1869.[97] Several years later, Enoch Wines was able to report that "the sentences of young offenders are wisely regulated for their amendment; they are not absurdly shortened as if they signified only so much endurance of vindictive suffering."[98]

Since the child-savers professed to be seeking the "best interests" of their "wards" on the basis of corporate liberal values, there was no need to formulate legal regulation of the right and duty to "treat" in the same way that the right and duty to punish had been previously regulated. The adversary system, therefore, ceased to exist for youth, even as a legal fiction.[99] The myth of the child-saving movement as a humanitarian enterprise was based partly on a superficial interpretation of the child savers' rhetoric of rehabilitation and partly on a misconception of how the

[94]*Ibid.*, pp. 310, 421.
[95]*Ibid.*, pp. 389–408.
[96]*Ibid.*
[97]Peirce, *op. cit.*, p. 312.
[98]Enoch Wines, *op. cit.*, p. 81.
[99]On informal cooperation in the criminal courts, see Jerome H. Skolnick, "Social Control in the Adversary System," 11 *Journal of Conflict Resolution* (March, 1967), pp. 52–70.

child savers viewed punishment. While it is true that they advocated minimal use of corporal punishment, consider-able evidence suggests that this recommendation was based on managerial rather than moral considerations. William Letchworth reported that "corporal punishment is rarely inflicted" at the State Industrial School in Roches-ter because "most of the boys consider the lowering of their standing the severest punishment that is in-flicted."[100] Mrs. Glendower Evans, commenting on the decline of whippings at a reform school in Massachusetts, concluded that "when boys do not feel themselves impris-oned and are treated as responsible moral agents, they can be trusted with their freedom to a surprising de-gree."[101] Officials at another state industrial school for girls also reported that "hysterics and fits of screaming and of noisy disobedience, have of late years become un-known. . . ."[102]

The decline in the use of corporal punishment was due to the fact that indeterminate sentencing, the "mark" or "stage" system of rewards and punishments, and other techniques of "organized persuasion" were far more effective in maintaining order and compliance than cruder methods of control. The chief virtue of the "stage" system, a graduated system of punishments and privi-leges, was its capacity to keep prisoners disciplined and submissive.[103] The child savers had learned from industri-alists that persuasive benevolence backed up by force was a far more effective device of social control than arbitrary displays of terrorism. Like an earlier generation of penal reformers in France and Italy, the child-savers stressed the efficacy of new and indirect forms of social control as a "practical measure of defense against social revolution as well as against individual acts."[104]

[100]Committee on the History of Child-Saving Work, op. cit., p. 20.
[101]Ibid., p. 237.
[102]Ibid., p. 251.
[103]Rusche and Kirchheimer, op. cit., pp. 155–156.
[104]Ibid., p. 76. For a similar point, see American Friends Service Committee, op. cit., p. 33.

Although the child-saving movement had far-reaching consequences for the organization and administration of the juvenile justice system, its overall impact was conservative in both spirit and achievement. The child-savers' reforms were generally aimed at imposing sanctions on conduct unbecoming "youth" and disqualifying youth from the benefit of adult privileges. The child savers were prohibitionists, in a general sense, who believed that social progress depended on efficient law enforcement, strict supervision of children's leisure and recreation, and enforced education. They were primarily concerned with regulating social behavior, eliminating "foreign" and radical ideologies, and preparing youth as a disciplined and devoted work force. The austerity of the criminal law and penal institutions was only of incidental concern; their central interest was in the normative outlook of youth, and they were most successful in their efforts to extend governmental control over a whole range of youthful activities that had previously been handled locally and informally. In this sense, their reforms were aimed at defining, rationalizing, and regulating the dependent status of youth.[105] Although the child savers' attitudes to youth were often paternalistic and romantic, their commands were backed up by force and an abiding faith in the benevolence of government.

The child-saving movement had its most direct impact on the children of the urban poor. The fact that "troublesome" adolescents were depicted as "sick" or "pathological," imprisoned "for their own good," addressed in paternalistic vocabulary, and exempted from criminal law processes, did not alter the subjective experiences of control, restraint, and punishment. It is ironic, as Philippe Aries observed in his historical study of European family life, that the obsessive solicitude of family, church, moralists, and administrators for child welfare served to deprive children of the freedoms which they had previously

[105]See, generally, Frank Musgrove, *Youth and the Social Order* (London: Routledge and Kegan Paul, 1964).

shared with adults and to deny their capacity for initiative, responsibility, and autonomy.[106]

The child savers' rhetoric of benevolence should not be mistaken for popular, democratic programs. Paternalism was a typical ingredient of most reforms in the Progressive era, legitimizing imperialism in foreign policy and extensive state control at home. Even the corporate rich, according to William Appleman Williams, "revealed a strikingly firm conception of a benevolent feudal approach to the firm and its workers" and "were willing to extend—to provide in the manner of traditional beneficence—such things as new housing, old age pensions, death payments, wage and job schedules, and bureaus charged with responsibility for welfare, safety, and sanitation."[107] But when benevolence failed—in domestic institutions such as schools and courts or in economic policies abroad—government officials and industrial leaders were quick to resort to massive and overwhelming force.[108]

This is not to suggest that the child savers and other Progressive movements did not achieve significant reforms. They did in fact create major changes. In the arena of criminal justice they were responsible for developing important new institutions that transformed the character of the administration of juvenile justice. But these reforms, to use Andre Gorz's distinctions, were "reformist" rather than "structural":[109]

[106]Philippe Ariès, *Centuries of Childhood: A Social History of Family Life* (New York: Vintage Books, 1965).

[107]Williams, *op. cit.*, p. 382.

[108]On benevolence and repression in foreign policy, see Felix Greene, *The Enemy: What Every American Should Know about Imperialism* (New York: Vintage Books, 1971). For examples of domestic repression, see William Preston, Jr., *Aliens and Dissenters: Federal Suppression of Radicals, 1903–1933* (New York: Harper Torchbooks, 1966) and Jacobus tenBroek, Edward N. Barnhart and Floyd W. Matson, *Prejudice, War and the Constitution* (Berkeley: University of California Press, 1968).

[109]Andre Gorz, *Strategy for Labor: A Radical Proposal* (Boston: Beacon Press, 1964), p. 8.

[S]tructural reform ... does not mean a reform which rationalizes the existing system while leaving intact the existing distribution of powers; this does not mean to delegate to the (capitalist) State the Task of improving the system.

Structural reform is by definition a reform implemented or controlled by those who demand it. Be it in agriculture, the university, property relations, the region, the administration, the economy, etc., a structural reform *always* requires the creation of new centers of democratic power. Whether it be at the level of companies, schools, municipalities, regions, or of the national Plan, etc., structural reform always requires a *decentralization* of the decision making power, a *restriction on the powers of State or Capital,* an *extension of popular power,* that is to say, a victory of democracy over the dictatorship of profit.

By this definition, then, the child-saving movement was a "reformist reform." It was not controlled by those whom it was supposed to benefit; it did not create new centers of democratic power; it extended and consolidated the powers of the state; and it helped to preserve existing economic and political relationships.

3. Counseling and Cultural Perspectives on Hardcore Youth Unemployment*

ROBERT C. FORTHMAN

Jobs have long been seen as a panacea for many social problems. It is a cliche that poverty and its effects would vanish once employment opportunities were provided. Forthman's observations seriously question this conclusion. He shows how unemployment has become a way of life for an identifiable sub-culture. The criminal justice system appears to provide the framework for identity transvaluations, rather than jobs.

The culture of poverty concept of Oscar Lewis is given strong support. The inability to profit from counseling, from vocational training, and from increased opportunities reflects a systemic, structural feature of the subculture. I have pointed out how prolonged participation in the culture of poverty has predictable cognitive outcomes in terms of such work-related attributes as time-perspective, lan-

*The author wishes to express his appreciation to Kermit Wiltse, Lydia Rapoport, and Carl Werthman for their assistance with the original dissertation, on which this article is based. The research was also supported by the School of Social Welfare, University of California, Berkeley; the National Institute of Mental Health; and the Manpower Administration, U.S. Department of Labor Grant Number 91-05-70-22 under the authority of Title I of the Manpower Development and Training Act of 1962.

*guage codes, and locus of control. (See Sarbin, T. R.
The culture of poverty, social identity and cognitive
outcomes. In V. L. Allen (Ed.), Psychological factors
in poverty. Chicago: Markham, 1970.) Forthman has
suggested that unemployability is a predictable social outcome for youth in a particular subculture of
poverty. Systemic binds rather than individual dispositions make up the context of unemployability.*

There has been considerable discussion over the past
few years about the cause and cure of our high youth
unemployment rate, which currently involves about 3.4
million youngsters between 16 and 24 years of age. This
study was focused on examining the sociopsychological
and cultural aspects, and response to counseling of an
unemployed low-income white youth population. Efforts
to assist such youth during the 1960s into satisfactory jobs
had not been particularly successful. Impressed with the
gains made by self-help groups in the civil rights, alcohol,
and drug addiction areas, the author wanted to test the
possibility of establishing a self-help peer group for unemployed adolescents, as well as using such a group as an
entering wedge for studying their employment problems
and the youth culture. These dual aims seemed to fit
nicely with the use of an action-research design to secure
an "insider's view" of the unemployment situation, as
well as of the wider community in which the youth lived.

THE COMMUNITY

The community studied was San Pablo, located in Western Contra Costa County on the San Francisco Bay in
Northern California. This particular town was selected
because of its proximity to Berkeley and its high percentage of low-income whites. While census data indicated
the low economic status of the population, it did not explain the important historical antecedents.

During World War II San Pablo was an unincorporated area with extensive cheap housing and served as a bedroom community for war workers in the Richmond shipyards just a few miles south. High wages for unskilled jobs in the shipyards attracted large numbers of workers, many of whom migrated into the area from rural southern states. As a result of this influx, the population of San Pablo jumped from 2000 to 18,000 between 1940 and 1950. Gradually the town took on a predominantly southern white flavor that resulted in the effective exclusion of potential black residents. After the war, the shipyards closed and the unskilled southern white population living in San Pablo began seeking other types of employment. Some were successful, but many found themselves drifting into poverty and on welfare. By 1960 the town had 25,000 residents of which 4000 lived on incomes under $4000 per year. Census tract 68 in San Pablo showed an unemployment rate then of 15 percent, which included the Pine Area, a section of the town noted for its multiproblem families and history of violence. This particular community included a population of 2800 families, 24 percent of which lived on incomes of less that $3000 per year. Children and youth under 21 years of age comprised nearly one-third of the population, and there was an extensive kinship system whereby many of the families were related by blood or marriage.

INSTITUTIONS AND AGENCIES

Based on interviews with both youth and adult Pine Area residents of San Pablo, it appeared that the most important agencies serving the community were law enforcement, health and welfare, employment, and the schools. Interestingly, within the law enforcement system there was considerable variation in the status accorded to the various components. Police were ranked the lowest, probation and parole officers were ranked intermediate, and judges the highest. In the health and welfare system, all the components were accorded low status, whether they were social workers, nurses, doctors, or administrators. Teachers in the public schools were also considered to have low status; and the local public employment office did not fare much better. The youth studied had no confidence that significant job help could be secured from that agency. Part of this problem became understandable when it was learned that the local labor market was characterized by a year-round surplus of unskilled workers along with available jobs requiring extensive training and/or experience.

Not everyone, however, blamed the local labor market for the situation confronting the hardcore youth in San Pablo. A variety of civic leaders, businessmen, and professionals attributed the major cause for the youth's unemployment to personal factors such as lack of motivation, inadequate work habits, high absentee rates, short-term interest in employment after certain minimal amounts of money had been earned, long records of arrest and violence on and off the job, more interest in "easy money" from crime rather than hard work, etc. These opinions of employed adults in the area stood in sharp contrast to the views of the unemployed youths themselves. Dealing with this contradiction, however, requires an explanation of why and how the data were gathered.

METHODOLOGY

An adequate understanding of these unemployed youth must rest on knowledge of both the objective facts and the subjective interpretation of these events. For the latter purpose, participant observation was used in the way defined by Severyn Bruyn (1966) as a "... study of human meanings and how they are revealed in the context of society." And, as indicated, the group was mainly male, hardcore unemployed white youth—"hardcore" referring to a variable, attenuated relationship that resists sharp definition as to whether the individual is either "in" or "out" of the labor market. The concept includes both internal and external factors, involving the discouraged worker, the involuntary part-time employee, the job hopper, poor access to jobs, high entry requirements, reduced number of job openings, etc.

Another sensitizing concept used was the "culture of poverty," as originally described by Oscar Lewis (1966). By age six or seven the attitudes of despair and futility can be so deeply etched into the personality of the slum-raised child that he is effectively prevented from taking advantage of real social, educational, and economic opportunities, should they be available to him later in life.

Other concepts employed in the study were more analytical in nature, such as methods of "interpretation," or the process of translating actual experiences into symbolic form suitable for sharing with peers. When the peer group understands the experience as intended by the communicator, then the meaning has become "concretized," which Bruyn (1966, p. 29) defines as a process for ". . . identifying and illustrating particular symbolic meanings which are significant to the culture being studied . . ." On a higher level of abstraction, it is possible to consider statements of value, value hierarchies, formal design of the culture, or how it is supposed to operate. And then, of course, there is the matter of how it actually operates (Bruyn, 1963, p. 269).

The methods for studying the unemployed youth in San Pablo included discovery, observation, description, and analysis. Locating the population desired for study through referrals of local social agencies proved unproductive, possibly because neither the agencies nor the hardcore youth had much interaction. A better method evolved from door-to-door canvassing and walking the streets in the Pine Area, keeping alert for small groups of youth lounging around street corners in the business section or working on cars in front of their houses. As a friendly relationship was established with a few informants, it became easier to get to know the other youngsters within their circle of friends. This author explained that he was a doctoral student studying youth employment problems in the community and that he had funds from the Department of Labor to pay for two-hour weekly group counseling sessions for youth who were unemployed and interested in getting a job. Part of the "contract" also included being available for placement assistance at other times during the week. In order to encourage continuity of attendance at the group meetings, the hourly "wage" was increased from $2.00 on the first meeting to $2.25 on the second up to a maximum of $2.50 on the third and subsequent consecutive meetings. If a meeting was missed, the participant dropped back to the $2.00 beginning rate. Among the youth participating, it became a matter of status to stay at the maximum rate as long as possible, and those who missed a meeting or two and had to drop back to the lowest rate got teased for being paid less.

These two-hour group sessions were tape recorded and content analyzed. They provided a rich source of data about the youths and were supplemented by other types of observation in their homes, on the streets, and during regular placement trips with them to employers. The author used his own car and usually took four to six youths with him on each excursion, some of which involved trips to San Francisco, Vallejo, Oakland, Fremont, and points in between.

Description of data collected outside of the group sessions was recorded in field notes. Later, all of the data, including the field notes and typescripts of group sessions, was edited and summarized on cards that were then classified by subject matter in much the same way as described by Herbert Gans (1962, p. 346) in his study of residents of West End Boston. Special attention was paid to attitudinal changes with respect to employability and actual behavior on the job for youth who were placed in employment after the project started.

LAUGHTER AND HUMOR

As beginning data was accumulated, this author experienced a jolting culture shock that almost led to the abandonment of the entire project. One of the few pleasant factors that encouraged continuation with the study was the humor and comedy inherent in the youth's experience. It may have been that attempting to understand the culture by way of issues related to employment and the work ethic—reasonable as such seemed to the author—was simply incomprehensible to the youth being studied. Rather, the early subjective experience of mutual understanding between the author and youth took this different route related to humor, mirth, fun, gaming, ridicule, mocking, and the like. Ultimately, this process opened up another powerful sensitizing method for observing and understanding many aspects of the culture. For example, a primary way of relating to employers seemed to be based on playing tricks and putting them down, a contest that the youth could "win" even though the result was loss of the job. A similar playful and mocking relationship existed with the police whereby the game rules of the youth made it possible for them to ridicule authority figures and put them down, no matter what the legal outcome of the contest. The process of securing secondary gains from participation within the criminal justice system showed how a social institution designed to deter antisocial behavior actually functioned to encourage and reward criminal acts. The way to secure status and reputation in this culture was to start by having a probation officer and later to "graduate" to the California Youth Authority and finally get "postgraduate" experience in one of the state prisons, preferably San Quentin, where many of the local role models either were or had been incarcerated.

The interplay of humor and ridicule explicated the culture in another way by showing that it is far more complex than might be implied by a simple reversal of middle-class values. The group observed was conflict-ridden, with aspects of both lower- and middle-class values straining against each other in shifting patterns, depending on the whims of the individuals involved. Observing the jesting and taunting relationships between peers gave this author a neutral position where someone else, for a change, was the subject of searching scrutiny and the transactions could be watched with minimal observer interference.

GENERAL METHODS OF OBSERVATION

During the initial exploratory phase of the study, June 1968 through May 1969, various interested adults in Richmond and San Pablo were interviewed to determine their opinions about the high youth unemployment rate. Then, from June to December 1969, this author began working directly with the youth in San Pablo and went through a period of rigorous testing by them to determine the real intentions of the project. The most common beliefs about the author's true role included narcotic agent, police informer, minister, or "do-gooder." By December, many of the youth seemed to find the role of university doctoral student studying employment problems a little more credible. Factors that may have lent support to this latter role definition involved a toughening up process undergone by the author where increasing limits were set, such as no more small "loans" of money, and the weekly group meetings were moved from the San Pablo Public Library to the home of one of the older participants who happened to be a strong role model for a number of the youth. This employed family man was also helpful in setting effective limits on aggressive behavior during group meetings, sometimes ejecting unruly members physically. Since it was his private home, the group accepted his authority, and also he was older, bigger, and tougher than the others. Once in a while he mentioned the loaded shotgun he kept in the front room closet.

Every possible circumstance was capitalized on for studying the youth. Meals were eaten with their families, they were visited in the Martinez jail and at the sheriff's rehabilitation facility at Clayton; they were accompanied to court at Oakland and at Martinez; the author went to the welfare, probation, and employment departments at various locations in Contra Costa County; and even to a local funeral after one of the neighbors was murdered. Besides their relationships to the wider community institutions, particular attention was paid to their use of language, this being so important to an understanding of the central meanings and themes of the culture. Because of the local southern dialects used, as well as the special meanings of certain words, it took several months to gain a sense of familiarity with their language. Tape recording the group interviews was helpful because it permitted the reexamination of certain words, phrases, and transactions within context.

YOUTH PERSPECTIVE

As indicated earlier, the status of being unemployed was *not* a very useful concept in understanding the major concerns of the youth. What did prove to be one of the most vital interests of these young men was the topic of cars. Boys and girls from other neighborhoods were not identified by their names, but by the make, model, and "badness" of the cars they drove. Not only were automobiles a favorite conversation topic, but they constituted major entry points within the culture to the criminal justice system, whether from stealing the cars or "boosting" necessary parts, acquiring speeding tickets, or from driving without a valid license or insurance. Once in jail for unpaid fines, the inmates could "work off" the money owed by "doing" a certain amount of time. This type of "employment" seemed far more natural to them than regular competitive employment outside of the jail, a distinction further accentuated by the high status associated with being in custody as opposed to the low status of merely being in a "rinky-dink" job. The police were thoroughly despised, but it was noted that during job hunting excursions the youth invariably requested that the author pull his car over alongside a patrol car so that the youth could chat with the officer on duty. This ambivalent relationship that included some attraction for the police seemed to be another reason for continued involvement with the criminal justice system. Many of these boys had no father in their home. One of the older youth mentioned that his mother had been a prostitute and the degree to which he had resented her male clients. This particular youth was one of the most aggressive in the group with an explosive anger and a reputation for assaulting smaller, younger boys. That he suffered status anxiety seemed apparent for various reasons, including the incident when he introduced the author to his probation officer as "my assistant." Although the tougher fighters were generally respected, this individual was not. Eventually he had to be dropped from the group because of assaulting one of the smaller boys during a meeting.

Another major theme besides toughness was the idea of meeting and wooing the girls, although the term used was not that polite. By current standards of the women's liberation movement, these boys were chauvinistic. They had many jokes about rape, statutory or otherwise. Several of them had fathered children out of wedlock, a fact that was viewed by various group members in contrasting lights. Generally, however, birth control was seen as the girl's responsibility and abortion was considered wrong, regardless of parental circumstances. How to meet new girls was a constant problem, especially for fellows who had acquired a reputation for getting them pregnant.

Along with their interest in girls, one of the few, if not only, advantages of going to school was that it provided a chance to mingle with the opposite sex. In almost every other respect, however, education was seen as dehumanizing. Teachers were only interested in the paycheck and the subjects taught had no earthly value. It is true that some of the youth were illiterate, and one fifteen year old was teased because he could not tell time. The most bitter complaint about schools seemed to involve self-discipline and control, for which these youth had not had much preparation in their homes. Parents would call the police when their sons got out of hand; teachers in the local primary and secondary schools had little recourse but to expel them when the verbal and physical behavior became intolerable. Ironically, these expulsions constituted a substantial reward for youth who did not want to go to school in the first place. As noted earlier with the criminal justice system, the school's ultimate "punishment" tended to reinforce the very behavior it was seeking to discourage. Increasing incidents at school and truancy led to the inevitable dropping out with more time on the streets and little prospect or inclination for legitimate employment.

Although some of the youth paid mild lip service to the value of employment, it obviously was an activity low on their list of priorities. For one thing, there were many easier and more exciting ways of making money. But, even if one were forced to work for wages, once the immediate financial needs were met, the job would be terminated one way or another. It is true, of course, that jobs were scarce and the ones that were available to these scruffy appearing young men were neither attractive nor well paid. The boys felt that some employers exploited them in various ways, but they also admitted stealing on the job whenever they got the chance, a practice they tended to justify because of the low wages paid and the authoritarian attitudes of the supervisors and bosses. Some of the participants put the blame for being unemployed on other members of the group for being lazy and totally unqualified, or as one youth put it: "I wouldn't hire you myself!"

The world of work was surprisingly vague to this group, so much so that some of the members knew where their father or mother worked but had no specific idea of what they actually did. Occupational goals tended to be vague, if they existed at all. When asked why they thought people wanted to work, the following reasons were given: pay off traffic tickets, buy clothes or a car, repay borrowed money, chance to meet girls, pass the time of day and stay out of trouble, and meet the expectations of others such as relatives, probation officers, and judges. Missing were references to bettering oneself or upward mobility, possibly because this did not appear to be a real option. Job hunting was seen as frustrating and unproductive, although there is some question about how much time and energy were actually devoted to it. Perhaps from the standpoint of the youth, they were making heroic sacrifices in this direction.

Their efforts, however, were quite dilatory. Their perception of the advantages of having a friend or relative already employed in the desired job location to act as a sponsor, however, did seem quite realistic. The state employment agency was considered of little or no help, as were the other local manpower programs. And the jobs available to them were viewed as unpleasant, dirty, undesirable, and low paying. The youth who did manage to secure employment were often terminated for tardiness and absenteeism, difficulty in getting along with co-workers or supervisors, or failing to comply with other job regulations, such as regular payment of union dues.

INTERPRETING THE YOUTH PERSPECTIVE

The fascination with cars and high-speed driving seemed consistent with the general search for various forms of "kicks," such as drugs, sex, crime, and "cops-and-robbers games" with police and the like. It would be a mistake, however, to conclude that these youths had lots of interesting and exciting things to do. Quite the opposite was true. Long hours of utter boredom waiting for something to happen seemed to be the general rule. The unending struggle against social norms and authority offered one type of escape from the tedium, the police being the major target of this rebellion. And the sense of social insignificance and injustice was partially assuaged, at least, by fighting in their underground guerilla organization aimed at harassing the establishment in every way possible. Converting society's ultimate form of punishment through incarceration in prison into a fundamental status symbol of achievement meant that the youth had the odds in their favor. Either way they could come out winners, based on their definitions of the conflict. Thus, locking these young men in detention made them heroes in the eyes of their peers, and the criminal justice system was transformed into a vast reward process where the assumed deterrent effect was nullified. This is one example of how some of the fundamental meanings of middle-class culture have been turned upside down.

The good life, which was within reach for these youth, was fun, excitement, sexual adventure, physical mobility, violence, and crime. From their standpoint, the unattainables were good social standing, education, desirable jobs, and what is involved in upward mobility. To avoid feeling sorry about the things they could never have, they simply devalued these unattainables and elevated the importance of the things they might hope to acquire, a very common type of defense mechanism. Thus, they could comfort each other and support the rightness of this type of solution since they were all in pretty much the same situation—not victims of poverty per se, but rather for living in a system favoring older and wealthier people.

The view of American society was highly cynical: every group was out to exploit others. No one was concerned about the general welfare of all Americans, and the government was totally lacking in legitimacy. True, it had the coercive power to force people, but not the qualities to encourage loyalty and respect. Within this context, the conventional ideas of right and wrong were recognized and even sometimes used against another person when convenient. But conventional morality seemed to have little binding power over actual behavior. Instead, the issues of coercion and force had more appeal than ideas of ethics. Perhaps adults in the community who had been successful in an economic sense by following the pre-scribed routes of education and good jobs had left, and the remaining adults were either examples of failure in terms of good legitimate jobs or they were crooks. At any rate, the youth had very few role models who could serve as guides for attractive law-abiding behavior.

They did not look forward to good jobs, but rather ex-pected to mix crime with poorly paid employment, sup-plemented by welfare between occasional trips to prison. Strangely, such behavior was seen as quite normal, except for the very rich. The youth had been socialized with experiences of chronic poverty, child abuse and neglect, sexual perversion, ill health, mental illness, violence, and social apathy that seemed to destroy their potential for basic trust in parents, community institutions, and the wider society. Their parents themselves were in continual conflict with the police, welfare, schools, probation, and other agencies, so the pattern of rebellion was set quite early. Perhaps this deep suspicion and wariness were nec-essary for early survival within this poverty culture. But, once established, there seemed little chance that the San Pablo youth would have later experiences that would cause them to develop a more positive relationship to the wider society. It looked, instead, as though their future would be mainly oriented toward the welfare and crimi-nal justice systems. Union members in the apprenticeship training programs reported very little success with this group for what appeared to these older men as lack of motivation. Probation officers indicated that the only way these kids got any attention from society was by getting into trouble. Growing up in San Pablo was seen as being subjected to gross humiliation and injustice—a degradation that generated a sense of exploitation, frustration, and determination to strike back—a slightly different theme than a simple bid for more approval and attention.

QUANTITATIVE RESULTS

Between May 1969 and August 1970 the author observed approximately 100 youths living in the Pine Area of San Pablo, 90 percent male, the majority of whom were between the ages of 16 and 19. Most described themselves as white, even though they had a strong admixture of American-Indian ancestry. The remainder of the group was composed of 25 percent Mexican-Americans and 6 percent blacks. About three-fourths of this entire group attended one or more of the weekly discussion meetings. A total of 62 group meetings was held, tape recorded, and transcribed; 19 of these meetings were content analyzed and showed the following topics to be of greatest interest to the group: jobs, cars, legal problems, sex, peer relations, drugs, and drinking. Average youth attendance at these meetings was 10 individuals. Approximately 75 youths received some specific form of job assistance such as individual counseling, placement, help in completing application forms, transportation, etc. Ten youth were assisted into training programs and about 50 secured jobs, some of which were of short duration. The number of direct contacts the author had with these individuals varied from one to 85, with the average being 30. Adequate data were gathered on approximately 50 youth, and were ranked in one of three employment typologies: extreme employment problems—27 percent, moderate employment problems—43 percent, and slight employment problems —30 percent. And a typical case example for each category was described. Because the third category with only slight employment problems seemed to be of less importance to the study, major emphasis has been placed on groups one and two, which composed 70 percent of the total population.

Cultural Aspects

The families of the youth from the first two groups presented a picture of extreme poverty, deprivation, illness, social disorganization, and major crime involving the youth, siblings, and parents. As indicated earlier, almost all the parents had migrated from southern states during or shortly after World War II and had brought many aspects of southern culture with them including strong antiblack prejudice. The youths' experience in the integrated local schools seemed to have little or no influence on their racism, nor did the strong civil rights movement that was securing publicity in the mass media during that period. These young people seemed to be encapsulated in an island of southern rural culture that effectively resisted assimilation by the schools, churches, social organizations, and other civic influences. This insulation may have been enhanced by the strong extended kinship system, which seemed to have more meaning for the families than other social structures in the community. Because there was such a high rate of unemployment and short-term jobs, it may be assumed that the kind of socialization that often takes place within an occupational context was lacking or ineffectual.

What surprised this researcher the most was the central role of the criminal justice system in the lives of the youth and their parents. It was as though the doors to all other institutions were closed, but this system had an "open door" policy that excluded no one. In San Pablo, the evening paper was often opened first, not to the sports page, but to the police blotter. Youths carried around news clippings that constituted their credentials and involved arrests, trials, and parole status from the Youth Authority.

During World War II when manpower was needed to build ships, their parents had important roles to play in the employment system. After the war ended and unemployment increased, many of them went on welfare, and finally their children were accommodated within the criminal justice system. The alienation of these youth can be described on the individual level, but there seems to be a cultural and historical aspect to it that is not adequately explained on that basis. For example, was it realistic to expect this southern rural white population to become assimilated into an urban labor market that experienced long-term increasing rates of unemployment? These families helped their country during a time of stress when it needed them. Like a sort of G.I. benefit program, their country might have returned the favor and extended special assistance to the families when they needed employment; instead, they received welfare. The War on Poverty was fading when this study was conducted, but even had it continued it is questionable that the programs developed had much to offer the youth of San Pablo. Some of them had been through the Job Corps several times, but still could not find or hold steady jobs.

Conclusions and Implications

Although various benefits were secured by some of the youths in the project, the major goal of improving their employability through a combination of individual and group techniques was not achieved. The most useful services provided were those actually requested by the youths themselves—help in securing disability benefits, transportation to court hearings, referral to drug detoxification centers, assistance in securing emergency medical and dental services, advocacy services in connection with welfare and drivers license applications, and the like. Providing these concrete services also certainly facilitated the study in that it helped in the establishment of an open and trusting relationship and also afforded excellent opportunities for observing the interaction of the youth with various adults, agencies, and the wider community. The youth that did secure employment usually did not hold their jobs very long for a variety of reasons related to their general life-style and frequent legal problems, transportation difficulties, and inappropriate behavior on the job. Efforts by the author to provide them with supportive counseling when problems arose before job termination were mainly ineffectual. Perhaps this resistance to help should not be too surprising in view of the difficulties these youths demonstrated in using any type of counseling, even under more favorable circumstances. The weekly group meetings never became productive counseling sessions although they did provide a wealth of information about the culture. And the group job hunting excursions to various employers were converted by the youth into recreational rather than vocational experiences, an agility that was observed in so many instances when the group interacted with outside social institutions and modified them to meet their own needs. The ability to extract needed resources from what was perceived as an alien, indifferent society showed some degree of social competency.

The Synanon and Delancey Street self-help models, however, proved to be inapplicable to the San Pablo youth studied because the author was unable to establish the minimum requirements for a solid self-help effort. The individual energies were like mercury; they seemed to go off in all directions with more satisfaction in tearing each other down than building something that would be good for the group. A colleague with extensive social group work experience visited one meeting and told the author afterwards that such a group in the agencies where he had been employed would have been dropped on the basis of being without substantial value for the participants.

It seemed that the vocational aspects of the project were not more successful because the effects of chronic poverty had undercut the development of normal social relationships and resulting values to such an extent that the institutions of family, school, and job were essentially alien and nonsupportive. Rather than viewing this as social disorganization, the youth culture could be considered a *new* type of social organization that represented the efforts of one group to extract the conditions necessary for survival from regular community institutions.

With all the critical moralizing directed at this group from representatives of the established social order, the fact that they could not be forced, tricked, or coaxed into being proper, conforming American citizens says something about the tenacity of their subculture. There is a tragic quality to this kind of conflict, though, where a small, embattled group of adolescents is absolutely convinced of the rightness of its position based on its experience, and the wider society is equally sure of the group's wrongness and need to be changed or punished. One way to resolve this situation seemed to be helping the youth into decent jobs. But it was not that easy. With the best of intentions and substantial social work effort, the author was not able to use improved employability as a bridge between San Pablo and affluent America.

Why was the reduction of this gap between two cultures so recalcitrant? Perhaps, in part, because it was the youth who were asked to do all the changing, with little outside help in terms of readjusted institutions and opportunities. As long as public opinion holds that these youth can be coerced into conformity, first through education and later through the criminal justice system, then this same bias will resist considering the possibility that naked force and power may never work. A more sophisticated approach might lie in the direction of enhancement of community "health" through modification of the basic socializing institutions. It seems quite doubtful that the mere expansion of job opportunities and manpower programs alone will resolve the alienation observed in the San Pablo youth. Their frustrations and hatred have been entrenched since early childhood, and their resolution would require effective intervention during childhood directed at family, school, and community institutions. Although limited in scope, Head Start programs are one effort in that direction.

That public funds will be spent on the kind of problems presented by youth in San Pablo is certain; the question seems to revolve around how these monies will be spent, which institutions will be subsidized, and how the results will be monitored. Present public policy seems to lean toward increasing support for institutions of social control that come into play late in the developmental process, such as law enforcement and correctional agencies. The experience in San Pablo leads to little optimism about this kind of approach for the population observed, or the social work-manpower model with which the project was initiated, for that matter. Perhaps a far more complex model for intervention is needed, one that combines individual, family, peer group, and community institutions, and policy modification or resource allocation in the areas of education, employment, and corrections. With an almost total lack of family policy, the other social and economic policies often seem to operate at cross purposes with each other. And an appropriate time span for such intervention would need to extend beyond a single generation. Whether this approach is feasible and would resolve the problems observed, remains to be seen. The phenomenon of hardcore unemployed youth, however, promises to be with our society for some time to come.

References

Bruyn, S. *The human perspective in sociology: The methodology of participant observation.* Englewood Cliffs: Prentice-Hall, 1966.

Gans, H. *The urban villagers: Group and class in the life of Italian-Americans.* New York: Free Press, 1962, p. 346.

Lewis, O. *La vida.* New York: Random House, 1966, p. XLIV.

4. Pretrial Interventions in the Criminal Justice System*

RONALD ROESCH

One aspect of contemporary criminology that has received a great deal of attention is pretrial intervention. Roesch introduces the reader to two forms: pretrial diversion and bail reform. Both of these legal processes had their origins in the failure of the traditional judicial system to recognize race and class discrimination. In a detailed review of available research on the effectiveness of pretrial interventions, Roesch points to a parallel between outcome research on pretrial interventions and outcome research in psychotherapy: treatments, therapists, clients, problems, and circumstances are all interacting variables.

The earliest, and continuing, involvement of mental health professionals in the criminal justice system has been the interpretation that criminal behavior is indicative of mental illness (Menninger, 1968; Shah, 1969; Szasz, 1963, 1970). The notion of rehabilitation follows from this interpretation, resulting in the often conflicting philosophies of viewing prisons as settings for punishment *and*

*The author wishes to thank Julian Rappaport and Edward Seidman for comments on an earlier draft.

rehabilitation. The indeterminate sentence is a direct effect of this conflict since it is primarily based on the mental health professions treatment and rehabilitation orientation. This practice allows offenders to be sentenced to prison for indefinite periods of time, usually within a minimum and a maximum range, and be released at an earlier time if the offender responds to rehabilitation. Patuxent Institute in Maryland is an example of the effect of mental health views on corrections. Staffed almost entirely by mental health professionals, Patuxent represents the ideal setting, according to many psychiatrists, for treating offenders. The indeterminate sentence is an assumption believed critical to Patuxent's success (Carney, 1974) since offenders are not to be released until they are "cured." This assumption continues to enjoy support even though it has not been empirically validated.

As Silber (1974), Kittrie (1971), and others have suggested, the interpretation of criminal behavior as yet another form of deviance in need of mental health intervention is based on humanitarian principles. It was, and still is to a large extent, viewed as a more morally and ethically defensible position to treat offenders rather than punish them, and one that would be more beneficial to the offender and society since it is assumed that treatment will be more effective than the usual methods of corrections. The idea that treatment is an effective method for dealing with offenders has recently come under attack. At least two major reviews (Bailey, 1971; Lipton, Martinson, & Wilks, 1975) have cast considerable doubts on the effectiveness of a variety of treatments in institutional and noninstitutional settings. The most sophisticated examination of group therapy in prison found that the therapy was unrelated to any of their measures of prison and postprison adjustment (Kassebaum, Ward, & Wilner, 1971).

The belief that the substitution of one form of social control (the mental health system) for another (the criminal justice system) will be more beneficial and humane is also suspect. For example, the practice of allowing some defendants to have their trials postponed because they are unable to participate in their defense *(Dusky v. United States)* is thought to be an important legal safeguard. Mental health professionals, typically psychiatrists, have been involved in the determination of competence to stand trial. The result for defendants found incompetent may not be humanitarian or much of a legal safeguard. Such defendants remain in mental institutions until they regain competency and are either returned to trial or the charges are dismissed. The length of detention may frequently be longer than the maximum sentence that could have been given (Roesch & Golding, 1977). Patuxent Institute is yet another example of how the treatment philosophy may be less than humanitarian. Persons committed to Patuxent frequently remain longer than they would have in a conventional prison. Other examples, such as detention in a halfway house versus jail detention, can easily be found.

The treatment interpretation is also based on the fact that as mental health professionals became involved in criminal justice they applied the training and conceptualizations that were part of their professions to their understanding of criminal behavior. Thus, the premise that criminal activity is rooted in psychological disturbance was not based on any scientific discovery but, rather, resulted from an application of the knowledge and skills of these professionals. The central problem is not that psychiatric or psychological treatment is not at all useful with offenders but that it has been misapplied and overapplied. It is certainly true that not all offenders will benefit from individual or group therapy, just as it is not true that all persons in the general population will benefit from these forms of treatment. As Robinson (1974) has argued, "every punishable act does not constitute a justification for involuntary therapy (p. 237)."

A noted Federal judge, David Bazelon, has commented on his doubts about the contribution of psychology to criminal justice (Bazelon, 1973). He was not questioning the expertise of psychology but the appropriateness of the application of this expertise in corrections. Bazelon argues that "psychologists have not produced any remarkable successes in the corrections field (p. 150)" and calls for a close scrutiny of their future role, if any. Paul Meehl (1970) has added that "the painful fact of the matter is that *we do not know how to treat, or 'cure,' or rehabilitate, or reform* criminal offenders (p. 4, italics his)." These statements will be debated for years. It is not the purpose of this chapter to try to resolve this issue, but instead to explore the potential involvement and contributions of psychologists in roles beyond those of traditional therapeutic interventions. The development of community psychology, for example, is at least partially based on a rejection of the individually oriented, traditional methods of clinical psychology and psychiatry. Community psychology's emphasis on prevention, analysis and modification of social systems (Cowen, 1973; Kelly, 1971; Rappaport, 1977), and the development, implementation, and evaluation of social innovations (Fairweather, 1972) represents a contribution to criminal justice that should be explored. It should not be viewed as a panacea but should be carefully evaluated at the level of underlying assumptions and values as well as outcomes, just as interventions based on other values and assumptions should be evaluated.

This chapter focuses on interventions in the criminal justice system that can occur at the pretrial level. Two interventions, bail reform and pretrial diversion, will be discussed in detail. Other pretrial interventions will be briefly reviewed.

BAIL REFORM

Change in the methods of securing pretrial release necessarily requires a change in the legal system. The traditional method of releasing defendants prior to trial is the setting of a cash bail. Defendants can obtain release by posting the full bail amount with the court or by paying a professional bondsmen a percentage of the full amount, usually 10 percent, who in turn guarantees the full amount to the court should the defendant not appear in court. If the full amount is paid by defendants, the entire sum is usually returned to them upon appearance in court. The ten percent paid to the bondsmen is forfeited, regardless of court appearance.

The traditional method of release has obvious disadvantages. Defendants who are indigent or who have low incomes typically remain in jail until their trial. Other defendants may spend weeks in jail while family and friends attempt to obtain the funds necessary to post bond. Thus, the traditional system is discriminatory against poor defendants.

Setting of bail is usually based on little information about defendants. The primary purpose of bail is to ensure the defendant's appearance in court. However, since little is known about a defendant the amount is based on the type of offense and prior record. Nonpecuniary factors that may be related to court appearance, such as community ties, are usually unknown, although many judges argue that they take these factors into account when setting bail. For example, Ebbesen and Konecni (1975) asked 18 judges to set bail on eight different case records that included information on age, description of crime, marital status, defense and prosecutor recommendations, prior record, and local ties. The judges were most influenced by prior record and local ties in this simulated study. But in actual courtroom observations of five of the eighteen judges, their decisions were almost exclusively based on the prosecutor's recommendation, which in turn was primarily based on severity of the crime.

Two types of system level changes which result in increased pretrial releases will be reviewed: point systems and 10 percent plans. Both represent significant changes in the legal system because they have altered the methods by which the courts release defendants prior to trial.

Manhattan Bail Project

The Manhattan Bail Project was initiated by the Vera Institute of Justice in 1961. Observations of the bail-setting process in New York City indicated that bail was usually set by the court with very little knowledge of the defendants. The amount of bail was typically based on the prosecutor's recommendation to the court, determined by the type of offense and prior record of a defendant. Release on recognizance (ROR) was rarely used (Ares, Rankin, & Sturz, 1963).

Project staff were concerned with collecting information about defendants which could be provided to the courts at arraignment. They developed an interview designed to assess factors they believed would be relevant in predicting a defendant's appearance in court. These factors were length of residence in the community, family ties, employment or school information, health, and prior record. They selected these areas because of their face valid relationship to predicting court appearance. Points were intuitively assigned to each area to indicate the relative importance of each factor. Defendants who have lived at their present address for a year or more were considered more stable and more likely to appear in court than defendants who have only lived four months at their current residence. Similarly, a full-time job in which the defendant had been employed for a year or more was weighted more heavily than was being unemployed. The current revision of the point system requires a score of six or greater for a recommendation of ROR. The possible range of points is -4 to 18. The information is usually collected in an interview, although a self-report questionnaire has been used in some communities. The information is verified, usually by telephoning references or employers. The entire time for the interview and verification is less than thirty minutes.

Studies of the effectiveness of the Manhattan Bail system uniformly show that the rate for failure to appear for

ROR releasees is as low and often lower than those defendants released on cash bond. Nietzel and Dade (1973) interviewed 80 defendants in Champaign County, Illinois during a one-month period, using the criteria established in the Manhattan Bail Project. Sixty-three (78.8 percent) of these defendants received recommendations to the court for release on recognizance, with the court granting release for 43 cases. Comparisons were made with 231 defendants arrested prior to the project and the first 100 cases completed immediately following the one-month project. Analysis of failure to appear rates for those defendants released on recognizance showed that the rate was lowest during the project (2.3 percent) as compared with preproject (10.1 percent) and postproject (15.8 percent). A significant aspect of the project was that it showed that the use of ROR increased during the project (55 percent) when compared with the pre-and postproject release rates of 34.2 percent and 38 percent, respectively. These data suggest that a point system can increase the use of ROR while ensuring that defendants so released will appear in court. However, there is some evidence to suggest (Bynum & Massey, 1976) that an increase in the ROR rate is associated with a decrease in the bond rate. Thus, ROR programs may not result in more releases or function as an alternative to incarceration. Those defendants released on ROR probably would have been released on bail.

A study of defendants released on their own recognizance in eight major cities (Wice, 1973) shows similar results. Most cities used the Manhattan Bail criteria in making release recommendations. In five of the cities the forfeiture rate was 3.1 percent or less, with two other cities having rates of 7.4 percent and 8.3 percent. One city, Chicago, had a forfeiture rate of 19 percent, which Wice (1973) attributes to a small staff with many defendants to interview, and little follow-up supervision. An interesting finding was that cities releasing the greatest percentage of defendants also had the lowest forfeiture rates. This finding is counter to the contention that decreasing the number of defendants released on their own recognizance, that is, being more conservative in the decision criteria, will serve to decrease the forfeiture rate.

As noted earlier, the Manhattan Bail criteria were developed on the basis of face valid factors assumed to be related to appearance in court. While there is a considerable amount of support for its effectiveness for those defendants released by these criteria, these findings ignore the possibility that defendants not qualifying because of insufficient points would also have appeared in court. The Wice (1973) study showed that, in all eight cities, less than one-half of the interviewed defendants were actually released on their own recognizance. In terms of predicability of the Vera criteria, this finding may suggest a high false negative rate. Gottfredson (1974) has conducted the only validation study known to the author of the Vera system. His study involved 539 defendants in Los Angeles arrested in late 1969 and early 1970. A variety of background information was collected, including personal characteristics, marital and family life, health, prior criminal record, and present offense. The first phase of the study involved the ability of the Vera scores to predict two criterion measures: court appearance and rearrest. The latter criterion was defined as arrest within 90 days of release. Correlations between the total Vera score and the criterion measures were low but significant due to the large sample size, but accounted for only two percent of the variance in the criteria classifications. Vera item analysis also showed only weak relationships with many of the items, such as family ties and residence, showing stronger linear relationships. The second phase of the study involved an analysis of the predictive utility of all information collected on the sample. The initial sample was randomly divided into two groups, the first group constituting a construction sample and the second a validation sample. Thirty-two predictors were subjected to a stepwise multiple regression analysis for each criterion. The multiple correlation coefficients were moderately high, ranging from about 0.40 to 0.45. However, when applied to the validation sample the multiple regression equations did not result in a better prediction than was possible with the Vera score. Gottfredson (1974) noted the need for establishing the reliability of the predictors as well as the need for examining the validity of the criteria measures and suggested the need for similar studies in other communities.

10 Percent Plans

The bailbonding industry has frequently come under attack. Defendants released in this manner do not recover any of the money paid to bailbondsmen when they appear in court. In cases of even moderately high bonds, such as $5000, this can be a substantial amount. The states of Illinois and Oregon have established an alternative that has eliminated the professional bondsmen. This plan allows defendants to post 10 percent of the total bail amount with the court. A refund of 90 percent of this deposit is returned to the defendant upon appearance in court. The total cost of release becomes 1 percent rather than 10 percent. Of course, this alternative imposes the same hardships on defendants with little or no financial resources but has the advantage of allowing financial incentive for court appearance to remain with the accused rather than a bondsmen.

Wice and Simon (1970) conducted a survey of fifteen communities that were divided into three categories depending on the type of release available. The three categories, each represented by five communities, were traditional bail, bail reform (utilizing point systems), and the 10 percent plan. Table 1 shows the result of this survey. Both reform and the 10 percent plan communities released a larger number of defendants than did traditional release cities. Further, the failure to appear rates, combined with re-arrest rates, were almost identical, regardless of form of release.

In summary, interventions designed to increase the use of release on recognizance or which provide alternatives to bailbonding business represent significant changes in the court system. The use of either method has resulted in more defendants being released prior to trial, without any subsequent increase in the failure to appear rate. The advantages to both defendants and taxpayers are numerous. Defendants may maintain employment and family relations and be in a better position to prepare a defense. The author (Roesch, 1976) has demonstrated that bail reform, as well as pretrial diversion, can result in reduced jail populations, and a consequent savings to taxpayers since future jail construction would be minimized or eliminated. It seems clear, however, that many defendants continue to remain in jail who could safely be released, even in communities that have bail reform programs. Point systems appear to be a method for legitimizing and encouraging alternative methods of release because they are ostensibly based on a more scientific quantitative system. Following the multiple regression model used by

Table 1   Comparison of Communities Using Alternate
Methods of Pretrial Release*

	Method of release			
	Percent released	Percent who used bondsmen	Percent obtaining release without bondsmen	Percent of those released failing to appear or rearrested
Traditional bail practice	64	86	14	17
Bail reform	77	62	38	16
Ten percent plan	85	3	97	18

*Adapted from data provided by Wice and Simon (1970).

form of social control will be substituted for another. The consequence of this is that it diverts attention from other alternatives, such as decriminalization of many crimes for which persons are now being diverted (Schur, 1965).

Most diversion projects also emphasize individual and/or group counseling, implying that persons who commit crimes must be in need of psychological treatment. While this may be true for *some* individuals, it is probably useful for only a very small minority of persons being diverted. The emphasis on treatment is another method of drawing attention away from other economic and social conditions that may be related to criminal activity. Placing the blame and focus of intervention entirely on the individual, as Ryan (1971) suggests, allows these conditions to remain untouched. Further, with the exception of a project in Hawaii (Narimatsu, 1973), diversion projects typically require some level of participation in rehabilitative programs in the community as a condition of diversion, apart from the counseling services provided by project staff. Data from the Hawaii project suggest that these mandatory services may not be necessary, at least in terms of reducing future criminal activity. Recidivism rates defined as arrest within a two-year period following referral, for 68 deferred prosecution cases selected during a 32-month period was 7.3 percent. This finding suggests a tentative hypothesis that for some offenders (in the Hawaii project there were largely first offenders charged with victimless or situational crimes) the critical factor may be the opportunity for dismissal of charges.

The remainder of this section will consider legal issues, selection criteria, participant characteristics, and evaluation of diversion projects.

Legal Issues

Several civil liberty and due process questions are involved in diversion programs. Judicial proceedings are postponed during participation, which may mean a delay of up to one year. Participants must waive the Sixth Amendment right to a speedy trial. Skoler (1974) and the American Bar Association (1974) have suggested that this right must be voluntarily and intelligently waived. Defendants must understand the available options to diversion, the nature of the program, and the consequences of participation, the potential unavailability of witnesses should proceedings be resumed, and the understanding that the right will again become applicable if charges are not dismissed. Balch (1974) is not convinced that these safeguards sufficiently protect defendants. He argues that "persons could be arrested on relatively weak grounds and then threatened with vigorous prosecution if they insist on their right to a speedy trial (p. 4)." This is an area of concern apart from the speedy trial issue as well. As with plea bargaining, the prosecution may coerce participation in diversion when successful prosecution may be unlikely. An additional safeguard would be the availability of defense counsel prior to signing the waiver. The ABA (1974) points out that when diversion occurs after formal charges have been filed defendants have the right to counsel. However, many diversion projects accept defendants prior to formal charges, a time in which defendants do not have a constitutional right to counsel. Nevertheless, the ABA (1974) argues that this is a critical prosecution stage and counsel should be available, both to protect the defendant and the prosecution.

Another legal concern is due process or equal protection of the law regarding selection into a diversion project. Of course, restriction due to race or sex would be patently discriminatory. Most projects do have exclusionary criteria that, while they may exclude certain classes of defendants, are apparently not illegal because they are not arbitrary. Therefore, a project could focus on first offenders or exclude certain offenses such as violent crimes. The issue becomes important when offenders who meet established selection critiera are excluded from participation for unspecified reasons. Most diversion participants are not referred from prosecutors or the courts. If eligible defendants are not referred or not allowed to participate, a case could be made that they were not afforded due process.

A final major legal issue involves the right to a hearing for diversion participants who are being unfavorably terminated. As will be shown later in this chapter, unfavorable terminations average about 25 percent, with some projects having an unfavorable rate as high as 50 percent. The consequence of an unfavorable termination is return to judicial processing, regardless of the length of diversion participation. Prosecution staff argue that failure is not held against a defendant in any subsequent proceedings. Given that the prosecution staff is nearly always aware of diversion participation, it can certainly be contended that unsuccessful termination will have some, albeit unknown, influence on the disposition of the case. The ABA (1974) has contended that a neutral hearing is essential to protect the rights of defendants. However, few diversion projects have provisions for such hearings, even though the reasons for termination are frequently vague or unspecified.

Characteristics of Diversion Programs

A survey of diversion programs was conducted during the spring of 1975. A letter was sent to the 50 diversion projects listed in the *Sourcebook in Pretrial Criminal Justice Intervention Techniques and Action Programs,* published by the National Pretrial Intervention Service Center (1974). This letter requested information on selection criteria, participant characteristics, and outcome data. Thirty projects replied, although three reported that no printed materials or data were available. Therefore, information resulting from the survey was available, in varying degrees, for 27 projects. In addition, data from three projects were available in the form of journal articles or other published reports. Thus, data were available on a total of 30 projects.[1] The following is a summary of the selection criteria used in these projects, and the demographic characteristics of participants.

Type of Charge. Information was available from 28 projects that specified the type of offense with which a defendant could be charged. This criterion was divided into three classes: misdemeanors only, nonviolent felonies only, or both. No project accepted participants charged with serious felonies, such as murder, rape, or armed robbery. Seven of the projects accepted persons charged with misdemeanors only, while three projects only included nonviolent felony charges. The majority of projects claimed they would accept both misdemeanor and felony charges. However, data on the type of offenses of actual participants indicate that this was a paper criterion only for many projects. For example, one project that purported to accept felons actually focused heavily on minor misdemeanor offenses. Over one-half of the participants were charged with shoplifting.

Prior Record. Prior record was listed as an exclusionary criterion for 29 projects. Thirteen projects excluded any defendant with a prior conviction. Five projects would accept a defendant with a prior misdemeanor conviction, while eleven projects accepted defendants with prior felony or misdemeanor convictions.

[1]Information was returned from Pima County Arizona; Project Intercept (three sites in San Jose, Vallejo, and Haywood, Ca.); Hartford, Conn.; San Bernadino, Ca.; Dade County, Fla.; Orlando, Fla.; Escambia, Fla.; Atlanta, Ga.; Kalamazoo, Mich.; De Nova (Mich.); Citizen Probation Authority (Flint, Mich.; Lyon County, Minn.; Anoka County, Minn.; Baltimore, Md.; Project Found [Baltimore, Md.]); Syracuse, N.Y.; Hudson County, N.Y.; Operation Midway, N.Y.; Portland, Ore.; Richland County, S.C.; Nashville, Tenn.; PIVOT (El Paso, Tx.); Boston, Mass.; Cleveland, Ohio; and San Antonio; Tx. In addition, data in the form of published reports were available on Project Crossroads (Washington, D.C.); Manhattan Court Employment Project; New Haven, Conn.

Age. The majority of projects (15) specified no age limit, eight accepted only those 26 years of age or less, while three only accepted persons less than 21. Although most projects specified no limit, the age of participants actually accepted suggests a focus on the youthful offender. Data on five projects which specified no age limit supports this position. Sixty-six percent of the Pima County, Arizona participants were 24 or less; DeNova's participants were 21 or less (64 percent); the Syracuse project under 21 group amounted to 71 percent of all participants. The other two projects showed similar percentages.

Race. Of course, no project specifically excluded defendants by race. Data from 16 projects indicates that the acceptance rates of whites and nonwhites approximate arrest rates for these groups. A little more than one-half of the participants in these 16 projects reporting data were white.

Marital Status. Consistent with the young age of the majority of diversion participants, results from the survey showed that most (72 percent) participants were single.

Education. Less than one-half of the participants in eleven projects reporting data had a high school education.

Employment Status. Unemployed or underemployed defendants were a priority for many projects. Consequently, almost one-half (47 percent) of participants in eleven projects reporting data were unemployed when selected.

Length of Participation. Only one project (Hawaii) did not require any program participation. The modal length of participation was brief, three months or less, but about one-fourth of the projects allowed participation up to one year and two projects had extensions granting participation for up to two years.

Evaluation

The conclusions of two extensive reviews of diversion projects indicate that very little is known about the effectiveness of diversion. Rovner-Pieczenik (1974) reviewed fifteen projects, concluding that although many projects reported positive effects, including low recidivism rates and increased employment, research design problems severely limit the ability to generalize the results. Mullen (1974) reviewed some projects not reviewed in the Rovner-Pieczenik work, observing that the "evaluations performed have been based on fairly crude quasi-experimental design (p. 5)."

There are two major issues that need to be evaluated before any conclusions can be made about the effectiveness of diversion. Diversion is viewed as an alternative to the usual court processing of certain offenders. Is diversion a better method of handling these offenders? The basic issue is whether diversion is more effective than traditional judicial disposition. Apart from defining effectiveness, basic research design would suggest the need for randomly assigned subjects to the two groups. However, there is one more issue that needs to be evaluated. It has been suggested that the most appealing and significant aspect of diversion is that it gets persons out of the criminal justice system before they have become labeled as offenders, *and* it results in no conviction record. It may be that removing certain defendants from the system by dismissing their charges may in itself be sufficient to achieve certain goals, such as the low rate of recidivism found in the Hawaii project (Narimatsu, 1973). These two issues suggest the need for random assignment of eligible and willing defendants to one of three groups. One group would be diverted and receive all services provided by the project, while a second group would be diverted but receive no additional services. The final group would be a control group of defendants processed through the legal system.

No diversion project has conducted this type of evaluation, although the Vera Institute of Justice is attempting to implement it in New York City. In fact, only one of the 30 projects surveyed used a randomly assigned control group. Three other projects used a comparison group of defendants selected from court records prior to the project who were matched with participants by offense, past record, and some demographic variables. There are several reasons that these comparison groups are in fact not comparable to participants. Court records are usually sketchy and typically do not contain information about employment and other demographic factors. Also, many defendants who meet the paper criteria for acceptance into diversion do not become participants, either because project staff believe they are not suitable or because some defendants chose not to participate. Thus, the potentially important variables of motivation and cooperation remain uncontrolled. While these design problems render conclusions suspect, use of a comparison group does at least allow for some between group comparisons. Sixteen projects in the survey made no use of any comparison group, reporting only descriptive data on participants or prepost changes in employment.

Many projects included in the survey did report data on the number of successful and nonsuccessful terminations. Successful termination means that participants satisfied the conditions of participation and had charges against them dismissed, whereas a failure is defined as defendants who had to be terminated from the project, because of rearrest or failure to comply with a project contract, and were returned to the court for further processing. The ratio of success to failures yields some information about the overall effectiveness of a project. Mullen (1975) reported that nine diversion projects included in her review had a combined failure rate of 24 percent. Results of the current survey show a similar percentage. The overall failure rate for 16 projects was 25.4 percent, ranging from a low of 5 percent to a high of 52 percent.

Two pretrial diversion projects that included some outcome data comparing participants and nonparticipants will be reviewed in some detail to illustrate the status and problems of evaluating the effectiveness of diversion. Dade County (Florida) was one project that used a randomly assigned control group of defendants eligible but not allowed to participate in the project. These defendants were referred back to the courts for prosecution. Eligibility requirements included no prior record, age of 17 to 25; being charged with a misdemeanor or certain nonviolent and less serious felonies such as grand larceny or car theft; consent of victim and arresting officer; resident of Dade County; in need of vocational, educational, or psychological assistance; and no present indication of narcotic addition. Petersen (1973) summarized data collected during an 18-month period in which 505 participants were selected. An additional 34 persons selected at random during the first year's eligible population served as the control group. At the time of the Petersen report there were 370 participants who had completed association with the project. Successful completion resulting in dismissal of charges occurred in 70 percent of these cases.

The control group was used only to analyze recidivism since, unfortunately, no other data were collected on this group. Prepost changes in education and employment are reported, but Dade County, like many other projects, only includes figures for successful participants. These comparisons should be regarded with a high degree of suspicion since one would expect successful participants to show more change in these areas. A more critical and appropriate analysis would include all participants, both successful and not, since these comparisons would yield data on the overall effectiveness of the project. The Dade County comparisons of preacceptance and three to six months completion showed improvements in percent employed full time (32 percent versus 58 percent) and enrollment in school (30 percent versus 42 percent).

The Dade County project completed a cost-benefit analysis comparing the cost of the project with court processing. They report a figure of $875 for traditional processing, but no method was given for the calculation of this figure. However, for the purpose of discussing the problems of cost-benefit analyses let us assume that this figure is correct. Project participation was estimated to be $695 per case. Petersen (1973) concluded that it was therefore less costly to divert a defendant than to use traditional methods. Several problems exist with this comparison. One, as Mullen (1974) pointed out, is that the diversion cost per case must be adjusted to account for the 25 percent of unsuccessful participants returned to court for prosecution. Mullen (1974) recalculated the cost per case and found that a more realistic figure would be $914 per case based on the added court costs of unsuccessful participants. Calculated in this manner diversion is more expensive. Both of these comparisons are misleading. Diversion does not cost less but, in fact, the costs should be added to the total costs of arrest disposition. The budget of the criminal justice system, including prosecutors, judges, clerks, and so on, remains constant. The fact that 100 or even 500 persons are diverted has little effect on the operating costs of the system. The cost per prosecuted case would actually increase slightly. The only savings to the criminal justice system that could result from diversion projects might be the reduction of the need for increasing staff.

As indicated earlier, the Dade County project used a control group to analyze recidivism rates. Nichols, Rockway, and Greenberg (1974) defined recidivism as any arrest between selection and the date of evaluation, two years after inception. Program participants (N=560) showed a rearrest rate of 19.8 percent compared with a 32.4 percent rate for controls. The use of a control group is a significant design improvement over other projects but one methodological flaw seriously limits the recidivism comparison. The control group was selected during the initial year of the project which means that they had been exposed to arrest considerably longer than participants. Therefore, the finding that controls were arrested more is not surprising.

The second project selected for review illustrates the problems inherent in using a comparison group. The Manhattan Court Employment Project (MCEP) began in 1967 as one of the first pretrial diversion projects. The focus was on the unemployed or underemployed (defined as earning less than $125 per week). Defendants between the ages of 16 and 45 were eligible if they were charged with an offense other than a minor misdemeanor or serious felony (murder, rape, kidnapping, or arson). Any defendant who had spent more than one continuous year in a penal institution was excluded, as were drug addicts and alcoholics. Participation was usually for 90 days.

During the three years of operation the project accepted 1300 defendants, representing about 2 percent of the yearly arraigned population. The median age was 19, indicating that even though older defendants were eligible, they were not selected. This may be due to the fact that many older defendants were excluded due to prior records. Most participants were single (74.8 percent) and either black (50.2 percent) or Puerto Rican (30.5 percent). Average educational level was 10.2 years. Project services included individual group counseling, job placement or training, or academic placement. Significantly, many of the counselors were ex-convicts or ex-addicts with backgrounds highly similar to participants.

Evaluation of MCEP involved prepost within group comparisons of participants and between group analyses using a group of 91 defendants selected from court records of defendants who appeared in court three months prior to the project and met the formal eligibility criteria. The project experienced a very high failure rate since slightly less than one-half of those accepted were successfully terminated. No explanation is offered for this unusually high failure rate. For most analyses the data were divided by year of project. Employment and income data included only successful participants. No employment data were available in the report on controls or failures. The analyses of pre- to postproject changes showed that employment and, consequently, income level were markedly improved for successful participants at completion. No significance tests were computed but the level of change for all three years was quite dramatic. As a measure of project effectiveness, however, these data are neither dramatic nor surprising. Since one of the selection criteria was unemployed or underemployed status, the result that persons who successfully complete the project were employed at a high rate is not unexpected. Again, an analysis of the overall impact of this project would require inclusion of failures as well as comparisons with a control group.

Analysis of recidivism compared successful and unsuccessful participants separately and included data on the comparison group. A 12-month follow-up of participants selected during the first 23 months of the project showed a 15.8 percent recidivism rate for favorable terminations and a 31.9 percent rate for the comparison group. The final report of the project (Vera Institute of Justice, 1972) argues that the project had a significant impact on recidivism. A more appropriate evaluation of the overall effectiveness of the project should combine favorable and unfavorable terminations. When the data are combined in this fashion one finds a 24 percent recidivism rate for the 214 participants and a 31.9 percent rate for the 91 subjects in the comparison group. This difference, although still favoring the project, is not quite as supportive of its overall effectiveness.

A further problem with the interpretation of these results is the use of a comparison group, a comparison that presumes that the two groups are comparable at least in terms of selection criteria. Zimring (1974) has presented evidence showing that a group selected from court records will not be comparable to participants. Zimring analyzed 201 MCEP cases that had passed the first screening (based on court records) and who were interviewed by project staff. Only 14 percent of this group actually participated in MCEP. The most frequent reason for exclusion was drug or alcohol involvement (20 percent). The voluntary aspects of participation resulted in 14 percent of eligible defendants rejecting participation. Based on these findings, Zimring suggests that a comparison group would be expected to include more persons with drug and alcohol problems and many defendants who would have rejected participation. Thus, the comparison group used in MCEP, as well as comparison groups used in other projects, may have a large number of defendants who are undoubtedly not comparable to project participants.

In summary, pretrial diversion represents an intervention that appears promising but has not been adequately evaluated. The paucity of data obtained as a result of the survey summarized in this chapter shows a lack of concern for self-evaluation. Most projects seem content to accept the assumption that diversion is an effective alternative. The lack of evaluation has not, unfortunately, hindered claims of success or less frequently, failure. Fishman (1975) recently suggested that diversion is not effective and should be abandoned in favor of other potentially important changes like preventive detention for violent offenders and speeding up the judicial process. This conclusion was based on a review of 18 different diversion projects in New York City. These projects had a combined recidivism rate of 41 percent. Fishman made some use of a comparison group but his conclusions were based largely on the recidivism finding across all projects. This type of analysis ignores the differential success rates of participants within projects. For example, two age groups in Fishman's study, 30 to 39 and 49 to 71, had recidivism rates of 29 percent and 24 percent respectively. An obvious hypothesis is that diversion may be more effective for certain offenders than for others. Research on diversion has failed to ask these more specific questions. The author (Roesch, 1978) has recently suggested that the current status of diversion research and criminal justice research in general, is analogous to that of psychotherapy research a decade ago. Many studies had concluded that psychotherapy was not effective (Eysenck, 1952, 1965; Shlien 1966). Critics of this conclusion took the position that the research methodology was inadequate, rendering suspect any conclusions about effectiveness of psychotherapy (Bergin, 1971; Paul, 1967). It was argued that the research questions were too broad (e.g., does diversion work?) and that the task of researchers was to ask more specific questions, such as that suggested by Paul (1967) and Kiesler (1966), in which it is argued that outcome research should be directed toward answering "*what* treatment, by *whom,* is most effective for *this* individual with *that* specific problem, and under *which* set of circumstances (Paul, 1967, p. 111)." Criminal justice research, including research on diversion, must begin moving in this direction. The research methodology that has developed within psychology can be a highly useful contribution to studying the process and outcome of change in criminal justice.

OTHER PRETRIAL INTERVENTIONS

In addition to bail reform and pretrial diversion several other pretrial interventions can result in significant changes in the operation of the criminal justice system. Space does not permit a lengthy discussion of these interventions. Interested readers should consult the references for more information.

The amount of time between arrest and disposition is one area in need of change. In some jurisdictions it may take up to one year before final disposition occurs. Five to six months appears to be the norm, if the defense does not request any continuances. Campbell (1972) and Hickey (1975) have discussed several methods for reducing delay, such as case screening, use of computers, and limiting the length of time by statute or court rule.

Creation of alternatives to arrest is another method of pretrial intervention. The issuance of citations or summons in lieu of arrest for certain crimes, similar to the issuance of traffic tickets, has been developed in several communities (Feeney, 1972; Maloney, 1974). This procedure has been shown to be a cost effective method, in terms of reduced police time and detention costs, which also results in high court appearance rates.

Palmer (1975) discussed the development and evaluation of the Night Prosecutor's program in Columbus, Ohio. Many complaints involving interpersonal disputes, such as family arguments, landlord-tenant disagreements, and neighborhood fights are filed by citizens in any community. In Columbus, the citizen filing such a complaint is referred to the Night Prosecutor's office. A session is scheduled in which all parties meet, mediated by a law student. Either party or the mediator suggests a solution, which must be acceptable to all parties. The results are impressive. An analysis of 1000 cases showed that only 20 were resolved by the filing of criminal charges. Only about two and one-half percent of 3500 cases resulted in a second complaint.

ROLES FOR PSYCHOLOGISTS

Several interventions at the pretrial level were reviewed in the context of potentially important roles in which social scientists, particularly psychologists, may become involved. Although these interventions could have a significant impact on the criminal justice system, they lack sufficient empirical support and therefore should not be unquestionably advocated. Psychologists have the potential for making major contributions in this area because of their perhaps unique skills among social scientists in the area of program development and evaluation. This role calls for a departure from the more traditional and questionably appropriate roles in which psychologists have typically engaged.

It is suggested that future directions for psychologists, as well as other criminal justice professionals, should focus on an examination of the values and underlying assumptions inherent in their interventions. Many interventions, especially those in institutional settings, have clearly had as their goal making the institution or system function more effectively with fewer disruptions. The controversial Project START in Springfield, Missouri is but one example of an intervention that was designed to change "unmanageable" prisoners so that they would be less disruptive to the system (United States Senate, 1974). The goal of Project START was to return more manageable prisoners back to federal prisons rather than a concern with preparing these offenders for their ultimate return to the community. The creation of Project START also allowed the blame for disruptive behavior to be placed entirely on the offenders, and thus avoided the responsibility of examining the prisons as a cause of disruptive behavior. The result was an attempt to change individuals within the system rather than the system itself.

It seems evident that if psychologists are to become more involved in criminal justice, we must become more critical of our roles. It calls for, as Fairweather (1972) and Campbell (1969) have proposed, an experimental approach to social innovation in which we try out innovative ideas, carefully evaluate them and retain, modify or abandon them on the basis of our evaluation. Strategies for conducting these evaluations must be decided upon before implementation of an intervention. If not, the result will be that, as in the case of pretrial diversion, we will continue the same approaches without ever knowing their effects.

REFERENCES

American Bar Association, Commission on Correctional Facilities and Services. *Monograph on legal issues and characteristics of pretrial intervention programs.* Washington, D.C.: ABA, 1974.

Ares, C., Rankin, A., & Sturz, H. The Manhattan Bail Project: An interim report on the use of pre-trial parole. *New York University Law Review,* 1963, *38,* 67–95.

Bailey, W. C. An evaluation of one hundred reports. In L. Radzinowicz & M. E. Wolfgang (Eds.), *The Criminal in Confinement.* Vol. III, New York: Basic Books, 1971.

Balch, R. W. Deferred prosecution: the juvenilization of the criminal justice system. *Federal Probation,* 1974, *38,* 46–50.

Bazelon, D. L. Psychologists in corrections—Are they doing good for the offender or well for themselves? In S. L. Brodsky (Ed.) *Psychologists in the criminal justice system.* Urbana, Il.: University of Illinois Press, 1973.

Bergin, A. E. The evaluation of therapeutic outcomes. In A. E. Bergin & S. L. Garfield (Eds.), *Handbook of psychotherapy and behavior change.* New York: Wiley, 1971.

Bynum, T., & Massey, C. The implementation of community based corrections: An exploration of competency goals of equality and efficiency. Paper read at the American Society of Criminology meetings, Tucson, Arizona, November, 1976.

Campbell, D. T., Reforms as experiments. *American Psychologist,* 1969, *24,* 409–428.

Campbell, W. J. Delays in criminal cases. *Federal Rules Decisions,* 1972, *55,* 229–256.

Carney, F. L. The indeterminate sentence at Patuxent. *Crime and Delinquency,* 1974, *20,* 135–143.

Cowen, E. L. Social and community interventions. *Annual Review of Psychology,* 1973, *24,* 423–473.

Cressey, D. R., & McDermott, R. A. *Diversion from the juvenile justice system.* Ann Arbor: National Assessment of Juvenile Corrections, 1973.

Cromwell, P. F., Jr., & Rios, O. G. Bond supervision: Implementing the Federal Bail Reform Act. *Federal Probation,* 1974, *38,* 30–34.

Dusky v. United States. 362 U.S. 402 (1960).

Ebbesen, E. B., & Konecni, V. J. Decision-making and information integration in the courts: the setting of bail. Paper read at American Psychological Association, Chicago, 1975.

Eysenck, H. J. The effects of psychotherapy: An evaluation. *Journal of Consulting Psychology,* 1952, *16,* 319–324.

Eysenck, H. J. The effects of psychotherapy. *International Journal of Psychiatry,* 1965, *1,* 99–144.

Fairweather, G. W. *Social change: the challenge to survival.* Morristown, N.J.: General Learning Press, 1972.

Feeney, F. F. Citation in lieu of arrest: the new California law. *Vanderbilt Law Review,* 1972, *25,* 367–387.

Fishman, R. *An evaluation of the effect of criminal recidivism of New York City projects providing rehabilitation and diversion services.* New York: New York State Division of Criminal Justice, 1975.

Gardner, E. J. Community resources: Tools for the correctional agent. *Crime and Delinquency,* 1973, *19,* 54–60.

Gottfredson, M. R. An empirical analysis of pretrial release decisions. *Journal of Criminal Justice,* 1974, *2,* 287–304.

Greenberg, D. F. Problems in community corrections. *Issues in Criminology,* 1975, *22,* 1–34.

Hickey, W. L. Depopulating the jails *Crime and Delinquency Literature,* 1975, *7,* 234–255.

Kassebaum, G., Ward, D. A., & Wilner, D. M. *Prison treatment and parole survival.* New York: Wiley, 1971.

Kelly, J. G. The quest for valid preventive interventions. In J. C. Glidewell, & G. Rosenbaum (Eds.), *Issues in community psychology and preventive mental health.* New York: Behavioral Publications, 1971.

Kiesler, D. J. Some myths of psychotherapy research and the research for a paradigm. *Psychological Bulletin,* 1966, *65,* 110–136.

Kittrie, N. N. *The right to be different: Deviance and enforced therapy.* Baltimore: Johns Hopkins Press, 1971.

Lipton, D., Martinson, R., & Wilks, J. *The effectiveness of correctional treatment: A survey of treatment evaluation studies.* New York: Praeger, 1975.

Maloney, P. J., Jr. An analysis of the citation system in Evanston, Illinois: Its value, constitutionality and viability. *Journal of Criminal Law and Criminology,* 1974, *65,* 75–86.

Mandell, W. Making correction a community agency. *Crime and Delinquency,* 1971, *16,* 281–288.

Meehl, P. E. Psychology and the criminal law. *University of Richmond Law Review,* 1970, *5,* 1–30.

Menninger, K. *The crime of punishment.* New York: Viking, 1968.

Mullen, J. *Pre-trial services: An evaluation of policy related research.* Cambridge, Mass.: Abt Associates, 1974.

Mullen, J. *The dilemma of diversion: Resource materials on adult pre-trial intervention programs.* Washington, D.C.: U.S. Gov't Ptg. Off., 1975.

Narimatsu, S. K. Deferred prosecution and deferred acceptance of a guilty plea. In *A prosecutor's manual on screening and diversionary programs.* Chicago: National District Attorneys Association, 1973.

National Advisory Commission on Criminal Justice Standards and Goals. *A national strategy to reduce crime.* Washington, D.C.: U.S. Gov't Ptg. Off., 1973.

National Pretrial Intervention Service Center. *Source book in pretrial criminal justice intervention techniques and action programs.* Washington, D.C.: U.S. Gov't Ptg. Off., 1974.

Nichols, R., Rockway, A. M., & Greenberg, B. Research supplement: Dade County pretrial intervention program. 1974 project evaluation and statistical analysis of recidivism and selected treatment variables by experimental and control groups and pre and post data comparisons. In J. Mullen, *Pre-trial services: An evaluation of policy related research.* Cambridge, Mass.: Abt Associates, 1974.

Nietzel, M. T., & Dade, J. T. Bail reform as an example of a community psychology intervention in a criminal justice system. *American Journal of Community Psychology,* 1973, *1,* 238–247.

Nimmer, R. T. St. Louis Diagnostic and Detoxification Center: An experiment in non-criminal processing of public intoxicants. *Washington University Law Quarterly,* 1970, *1970,* 1–27.

Nimmer, R. T. *Diversion—the search for alternative forms of prosecution.* Chicago: American Bar Foundation, 1974.

Palmer, J. W. Pre-arrest diversion: the night prosecutor's program in Columbus, Ohio. *Crime and Delinquency,* 1975, *21,* 100–108.

Paul, G. L. Strategy of outcome research in psychotherapy. *Journal of Consulting Psychology,* 1967, *31,* 109–188.

Petersen, T. K. *Metropolitan Dade County pretrial intervention project: Eighteen month report.* Miami, Fla.: Office of the State Attorney, 1973.

Pettibone, J. M. Community-based programs: Catching up with yesterday and planning for tomorrow. *Federal Probation,* 1973, *37,* 3–8.

Rappaport, J. *Community Psychology: Values, research, and action.* New York: Holt, Rinehart and Winston, 1977.

Robinson, D. N. Harm, offense, and nuisance: Some first steps in the establishment of an ethics of treatment. *American Psychologist,* 1974, *29,* 233–238.

Roesch, R. Predicting the effects of pretrial intervention programs on jail populations: A method for planning and decision-making. *Federal Probation,* 1976, *40,* 32–36.

Roesch, R. Does adult diversion work?: The failure of research in criminal justice. *Crime and Delinquency,* 1978, *24,* 72–80.

Roesch, R., & Golding, S. L. *A systems analysis of competency to stand trial procedures: Implications for forensic services in North Carolina.* Urbana, Ill.: University of Illinois, 1977.

Rovner-Pieczenik, R. *Pretrial intervention strategies: An evaluation of policy-related research and policymaker guidelines.* Washington, D.C.: American Bar Association, 1974.

Ryan, W. *Blaming the victim.* New York: Vintage, 1971.

Schrag, C. *Crime and justice: American style.* (National Institute of Mental Health, Center for Studies of Crime and Delinquency), Washington, D.C.: U.S. Gov't Ptg. Off., 1971.

Schur, E. M. *Crimes without victims: Deviant behavior and public policy.* Englewood Cliffs, N.J.: Prentice-Hall, 1965.

Seidman, E., Rappaport, J., & Davidson, W. S. Adolescents in legal jeopardy: Initial success and replication of an alternative to the criminal justice system. Invited address, 1976 National Psychological Consultants to Management Consulting Psychology Research Award. Meeting of the American Psychological Association, Washington, D.C., 1976.

Shah, S. A. Crime and mental illness: Some problems in defining and labelling deviant behavior. *Mental Hygiene,* 1969, *53,* 21–33.

Shlien, J. M. Cross-theoretical criteria for the evaluation

of psychotherapy. *American Journal of Psychotherapy*, 1966, *1*, 125–134.

Silber, D. E. Controversy concerning the criminal justice system and its implications for the role of mental health workers. *American Psychologist*, 1974, *29*, 239–244.

Skoler, D. L. Protecting the rights of defendants in pretrial intervention programs. *Criminal Law Bulletin*, 1974, *10*, 473–492.

Szasz, T. S. *Law liberty and psychiatry*. New York: MacMillan, 1963.

Szasz, T. S. *The manufacture of madness: A comparative study of the inquisition and the mental health movement*. New York: Harper & Row, 1970.

United States Senate, Committee of the Judiciary, Subcommittee on Constitutional Rights. *Individual rights and the federal role in behavior modification*. Washington, D.C.: U.S. Gov't Ptg. Off., 1974.

Venezia, P. S. Unofficial probation: An evaluation of its effectiveness. *Journal of Research in Crime and Delinquency*, 1972, *9*, 149–170.

Vera Institute of Justice. *The Manhattan Court Employment Project final report*. New York: Vera Institute of Justice, 1972.

Weis, C. W. *Diversion of the public inebriate from the criminal justice system*. Washington, D.C.: U.S. Gov't Ptg. Off., 1973.

Wice, P. B. *Bail and its reform—A national survey*. Washington, D.C.: Law Enforcement Assistance Administration, 1973.

Wice, P., & Simon, R. J. Pretrial release: A survey of alternative practices. *Federal Probation*, 1970, *34*, 60–63.

Willins, L. P. Community based corrections: Some techniques used as substitutes for imprisonment. *Capital University Law Review*, 1973, *2*, 101–125.

Zimring, F. E. Measuring the impact of pretrial diversion from the criminal justice system. *University of Chicago Law Review*, 1974, *41*, 224–241.

5. Corporate Violence: Research Strategies for Community Psychology*

JOHN MONAHAN
RAYMOND W. NOVACO
GILBERT GEIS

Community psychologists, no less than other professionals, have been bombarded with requests for solutions to the problem of interpersonal violence. The exclusive focus by the mass media and by social scientists on interpersonal violence has supported the belief that violent conduct is an outcome of "aggressive personalities," lack of frustration-tolerance, or a way of life among the lower classes. Monahan, Novaco, and Geis, in identifying corporate violence provide us with a new frame of reference for conceptualizing violence. They also suggest some interesting research strategies for the community psychologist.

Public concern with violence ranks among the most salient problems of American communities. One-half of

*We wish to thank Edward Cohen of the U.S. Senate Commerce Committee, John Hubbard of the Center for Auto Safety, Thomas Lalley of the National Institute of Mental Health, and numerous employees of the automobile industry, who understandably prefer to remain anonymous, for their help in the preparation of this chapter. They are not responsible for the conclusions we have drawn. We are also grateful to Lyman Porter for his advice on the study of corporate decision making, to Daniel Stokols for sharing his knowledge in social psychology, and to Theodore R. Sarbin for suggesting the relevance of Arthur Miller's play.

117

the population of the United States reports being afraid to walk home alone at night. Urban residents, women, blacks, and the poor express more than their proportional share of fear (Office of Management and Budget, 1973). Violence, indeed, represents the most frequently cited reason for dissatisfaction with one's community (Ittleson, Proshansky, Rivlin, & Winkel, 1974). In a society such as ours, where the sense of community is frail and elusive, safety has become a principal real estate commodity.

Behavioral scientists, including community psychologists, have responded to public malaise about street crimes. They have done so, as we shall indicate in this chapter, in ways conditioned by their disciplines' definition of proper subject matter and methodology. Violent offenders who commit offenses such as assault and rape can be readily located and easily studied. In prison, they have ample time and considerable inclination to break the tedium by cooperating in psychological investigations. In addition, perpetrators of "traditional" forms of violence are rather declasse—they generally are from strata lower on the social scale than scientific researchers and therefore offer no status or other hegemony threats.

Little argument can be mounted against the view that street violence represents a serious assault on the right of citizens to be protected from harm. However, the argument pursued in this chapter is that there are neglected forms of violence that also represent a threat to the personal integrity of innocent citizens. People are quite as dead if they are killed by smog, defective automobiles, negligence in the factory, or other forms of industrial and corporate malevolence as they are if murdered by an armed robber.

This dictum, patently obvious once stated, nonetheless takes on particular importance when considering the consummate neglect by community psychologists of corporate violence by forces and persons otherwise regarded as "legitimate" and "successful" members of the social system. Such neglect has far reaching consequences, including the fact that it perpetuates a growing belief that behavioral science operates in behalf of established power groups rather than in behalf of an ethic of impartial assessment and scientific objectivity.

The growing body of social science research on violence has included the study of biological factors (Borgaonkar & Shah, 1974; Moyer, 1973; Vallenstein, 1974), human territoriality (Austin & Bates, 1974), environmental cues (Berkowitz, 1974), social learning processes (Bandura, 1973), the effects of television (Comstock & Rubenstein, 1971; Feshbach & Singer, 1971), the prediction of violence (Monahan, 1976), and the treatment of violent offenders and persons with chronic anger problems (Halleck, 1975; Novaco, 1975). A host of sociological investigations has included the study of homicide (Wolfgang, 1958), rape (Amir, 1971), armed robbery (Einstadter, 1969), and subcultures of violence (Wolfgang & Ferricutti, 1967). Psychologists committed to the study of community problems have developed strategies for preventing violence, most of which have focused on the training of police in methods for the constructive handling of interpersonal conflict (e.g., Bard, 1976; Novaco, 1977).

The dominant concern in community interventions and experimental studies has been with *individual* or *personal* violence. Attention almost exclusively has been focused on violence as a conspicuous transaction between two or more persons. Yet a convincing case can be made that most preventable death and injury in this country is occasioned by actions more subtle than family quarrels or liquor store robberies. This chapter will argue that violence resulting from corporate decision making is more a threat to the public safety than street violence or family violence. We also will propose strategies whereby community psychologists, among others, may investigate and consequently affect corporate processes that have resulted in large-scale death and injury.

CORPORATE VIOLENCE

Corporate violence is defined as illegal behavior producing an *unreasonable risk* of physical harm to consumers, employees, or other persons as a result of deliberate decision making by corporate executives or culpable negligence on their part. To apply the term "violence" to such acts, as we are doing, is neither an exercise in metaphoric overkill nor a dilution of the concept of violence. Rather, it is an attempt to redefine the boundaries of the term "violence" to include phenomena that properly should come within its purview. Instances of violence by corporate institutions have escaped description as violent for at least three reasons: (1) the anonymity involved in corporate actions, (2) the sequencing of the violence that has sheltered corporate perpetrators from direct association with the injurious consequences of their acts, and (3) the fact that corporate violence does not lend itself easily to observation by social scientists. In this regard, their exclusion from categorization as violent has been a matter of convenience rather than one of logic.

The traditional behavioral science focus on personal violence is not surprising in view of some of its intrinsic characteristics. It is precisely this kind of violence that the individual citizen fears. Such violence is most commonly associated with an identifiable perpetrator. Corporate violence is more subtle and less conspicuous. As long as violence is defined in terms of conspicuous transactions between persons, the violence performed by social institutions and their agents is obscured.

Corporate violence may be viewed as a form of "white collar crime" (Geis, 1968; Geis and Meier, 1977; Sutherland, 1949). Sutherland coined that term in his classic analysis of the history of 70 of the 200 largest corporations in the United States. These companies had been convicted of an average of 14 crimes each, including restraint of trade, infringement of patents, and unfair labor practices. Due to inadequacies in reporting practices, these figures are surely a gross underestimate of corporate crime. Baumhart (1968), in a survey of 1700 corporate executives, reported that a majority believed that businessmen would violate ethical standards if they thought detection could be avoided. When the respondents were asked to rank each of five factors (company policy, industry climate, behavior of superiors, behavior of equals, and personal codes) for their influence on executive decisions, they were most likely to attribute ethical decisions to personal codes of behavior and unethical decisions to the influence of superiors and industry climate. When asked if they knew of unethical practices in their industry, four out of five executives affirmed the presence of generally accepted practices which they considered unethical (Lane, 1953). While these findings refer to corporate crime in general, rather than specifically to corporate violence, they provide insight into the ethical climate of American industry.

No reliable statistics exist about forms of corporate crime that result in violence. The principle source of crime data in this country, the F.B.I.'s *Uniform Crime Reports,* ignores corporate violators. It is estimated, however, that 200,000 to 500,000 workers annually are needlessly exposed to toxic agents such as radioactive materials and poisonous chemicals because of corporate failure to obey safety laws. And an unknown but undoubtedly significant portion of the 2.5 million temporary and 250,000 permanent worker disabilities from industrial accidents each year are the result of managerial acts that represent culpable failure to adhere to established standards (Geis, 1973, p. 183). A likewise unknown portion of the approximately 50,000 deaths each year on the highway are the result of faulty automobile manufacturing.

Virtually the only form of investigation of corporate violence has been the case study. Geis and Monahan (1976) report that between 1964 and 1968, 13 persons were killed in crashes of a light aircraft whose fuel tank construction was faulty. The aircraft manufacturer was informed of the defect at least three years prior to the first fatal crash. This initial warning was supported by follow-up tests and by customer accounts of fuel mechanism inadequacies that produced hazards in flight. Rather than repair the planes, the company gambled that crashes would be attributed to pilot error. Similarly, a propeller defect that caused a 1967 crash of an airplane in Ohio killing 38 persons was known to the manufacturer, the Allison Division of General Motors, but the company chose not to advise anyone of the problem (Johnson, 1972; Mintz & Cohen, 1971). Franklin (1969) reported that the mine involved in the 1968 West Virginia disaster had failed all 24 inspections by the Bureau of Mines in the previous five years, and was cited for 25 safety violations in the two years prior to the tragedy. Despite the profitable technological advances in the extraction of coal, the performance of the coal industry with respect to disaster prevention has been callously inhuman. Excluding deaths from disease, more that 120,000 men have died violently in coal mines during the last century. Brodeur (1974) details dozens of other such instances of fatal corporate negligence.

The most famous case study of corporate violence is Ralph Nader's (1965) *Unsafe at Any Speed.* Nader accused automobile manufacturers of building lethal cars and concealing their knowledge of death-dealing defects from the public. The roster of vehicular defects linked to passenger injuries is indeed appalling. Among the most vicious have been rear wheel tuck-under in the 1960 to 1963 Corvairs, brake failure in the 1953 Buick Roadmaster, weak rear suspension arms in 1965 Fords, faulty steering gear brackets in 1965 Chryslers, and original equipment tires that are highly susceptible to overload. These items are only a portion of a shocking catalog of hazardous automobile equipment sold to the public.

Even more astonishing have been the nefarious decisions by manufacturers to ignore discoveries by engineering research of hazardous defects, so that safety concerns become preempted by the exigencies of the marketplace. Manufacturers have both delayed and avoided recalls once an equipment defect has been recognized. The Corvair was marketed for four years before the stabilization problems in its rear suspension were corrected in an improved 1964 design. This delay occurred despite hundreds of consumer complaints regarding the Corvair's instability, repeated criticism from automotive magazines, and numerous instances of the loss of vehicle control by industry test car drivers. As early as 1956, Chevrolet's head of research and development noted in a patent application that the Corvair-type suspension had serious defects relating to the vehicle's tendency to roll over (Nader, 1965). The Corvair's problem was especially dangerous because the hazard materialized suddenly and occurred within normal speed ranges on sharp turns. The design defects were commonly known to highway patrol officers, who over the years had become adept at recognizing gashes in the pavement from the rim of the Corvair's collapsing rear wheel.

Perhaps due to the nature of its product, the automobile industry appears more prone to corporate violence than to "merely" economic forms of corporate crime; or, put less elegantly, it seems particularly likely to produce a higher ratio of killers to thieves than are found in other large industries. This is strikingly illustrated in the remarks of Alfred P. Sloan, then President of General Motors, concerning the possible use of safety glass in Chevrolets. Sloan wrote in correspondence submitted as evidence at U.S. Senate Hearings in 1968 and reported in Mintz and Cohen (1971): "Accidents or no accidents, my concern in this problem is a matter of profit and loss. . . . Our gain would be a purely temporary one and the net result would be that both competition and ourselves would have reduced the return on our capital and the public would have obtained still more value per dollar expended . . . you can say perhaps that I am selfish, but business is selfish. We are not a charitable institution—we are trying to make a profit for our stockholders" (p. 258–260). As Mintz and Cohen noted, safety glass is one of the most valuable protections ever devised against death and disfiguring injury from automobile crashes.

FACTORS UNDERLYING THE LACK OF PSYCHOLOGICAL RESEARCH ON CORPORATE VIOLENCE

If corporate violence is responsible for more preventable death and injury than is street violence, why have psychologists chosen to focus their research attention exclusively on street crime? Why has no one tried to investigate the "personality profile" of the corporate offender? Why are "early intervention programs" and "violence clinics" initiated in the ghettoes of Detroit, but not in the nearby corporate headquarters in Pontiac? Several factors appear to be acting in concert:

Definitional Boundaries on the Concept of Violence.
Psychologists are subject to the same perceptual biases as other people. Psychologists have the same pervasive tendency to fear death by mugging and to be sanguine about death by industrial smog as nonprofessionals. We tend to be more sensitive and alert to risks that are immediately identifiable. Corporate violence is not "seen" because definitional boundaries have been limited to personal violence.

Access to Data. Even if psychologists were able to transcend the cultural tendencies that diminish corporate violence as a social problem, research on the phenomenon would be stymied by a lack of access to relevant data. One can readily arrange for apprehended street criminals to take a battery of personality tests or participate in a treatment program. But how does a researcher obtain subjects from a major corporation? Indeed, the very word, "subjects," seems somehow out of place in this context. In addition, companies have a great deal to lose if their violent behavior were identified. They are thus without incentive to cooperate in research that may show them in a negative light. The few corporate violators who are successfully prosecuted are incarcerated for only a short time, if at all. University researchers, anxious to publish, live out the joke of the drunk looking for his car key under the lamp post, not because he lost them there, but because that is where the light is. Psychologists do research on street crime, not because that is where most violence is to be found, but because that is where the subjects are.

Access to Funding Sources.   Sources of funding are much easier to come by if one is interested in street rather than corporate crime. The history of psychological research has largely been the history of funding opportunities (Quinney, 1974). When the Veterans' Administration was a major employer of psychologists, journals were filled with research on back ward schizophrenics. When community mental health centers began to hire psychologists in large numbers, community problems began to receive empirical attention. Prisons hire psychologists to do research on violent inmates; however corporations do not hire psychologists to do research on violent executives. Virtually all of the millions of dollars allocated by the Law Enforcement Assistance Administration (LEAA) have subsidized research on street rather than corporate crime. Other federal, state, and private funding agencies have behaved analogously. Research institutes, which exist only so long as they can solicit grant funds, pursue projects that will enable them to continue functioning. Corporate violence has not been in this category.

Political Considerations.   Finally, we should note the radical critique of psychological and sociological research in the area of crime (Quinney, 1974). It is not coincidental, state the socialist critics, that a capitalist society would devote substantial resources to repress violent crime by the poor while ignoring corporate violence. To the extent that Calvin Coolidge was right—that "the business of America is business"—one would expect corporate czars to protect their own. Radical criminologists have claimed that corporate violence is part and parcel of the American economic system and cannot be changed until that system is changed.

The radical critique of behavioral science may well be misreading a general trait of power structures as a characteristic inherent only in capitalist societies. Virtually all entrenched forces work assiduously to maintain their power; it is only that some are more successful in this endeavor than others. No government system advocates, much less allows, acts deemed to pose a direct threat to its survival, and few power structures are above resorting to violence to "protect" themselves from external or internal threats to their continuance.

In this sense, perhaps the most attractive trait of the American ideology, in theory if not always in practice, is that it provides room for espousal and pursuit of non-establishment-oriented endeavors. The difficulty observed here is that through preemption, or by a failure of nerve, researchers often impose ideological blinders on their work, failing to ask hard, unpopular questions. Ironically, they thereby do a greater disservice to the values that they allegedly support than those persons who directly oppose such values.

PSYCHOLOGICAL RESEARCH RELEVANT TO CORPORATE VIOLENCE

While psychologists have not provided research insights into the problem of corporate violence, they have, as noted earlier, been prolific producers of research on individual violence and aggression. To the extent that similar factors operate in both situations, examination of selected findings in the study of individual violence can provide hypotheses to be tested in research on corporate decision making in regard to violence. Four important factors are readily identifiable: (1) conditions of reinforcement, (2) modeling influences, (3) diffusion of responsibility, and (4) depersonalization of victims.

Reinforcement. Aggressive behavior can be shaped and maintained by reward contingencies. The conditions of reinforcement may be either direct (Geen & Pigg, 1970; Geen & Stonner, 1971) or vicarious (Bandura, 1965). The instrumentality of aggressive behavior, i.e., its function in obtaining a desired outcome, is a powerful determinant of aggression and its intensity (Buss, 1963, 1966). By systematically rewarding compliance and punishing noncompliance, aggressive behavior can be brought under instructional control (Bandura, 1973). The obedient aggression demonstrated by Milgram's (1963) research followed from the subject's displacement of social values in response to the requests of a perceived legitimate authority. When the demands of the instructing authority are more immediate and salient than the demands of the victim there is a greater probability of an obedient response (Milgram, 1965). Economic contingencies bearing on decisions within corporations appear to define the situation as one that is especially conducive to the instructional control of behavior. Baumhart (1968) found that the behavior of a person's superiors in the company was ranked as the primary determinant of unethical decisions by executives. As one of his respondents put it, "The constant everyday pressure from top management to obtain profitable business, unwritten, but well understood, is the phrase 'at any cost.' To do this requires every conceivable dirty trick" (p. 132).

Modeling. Bandura's (1973) social learning theory of aggression designates that the acquisition and performance of aggressive behavior is a function of modeling influences that operate through processes of observational learning, disinhibition, and response facilitation. Although instigation to aggression via modeling influences is often demonstrated when subjects have been angered (e.g., Baron, 1971; Baron & Kepner, 1970), instigative effects of modeling do not require emotional arousal (e.g., Bandura, 1973; Hartman, 1969). This is especially relevant to corporate decision making, where anger is likely to be absent.

Diffusion of Responsibility. To the extent that aggressors can exempt themselves from self-devaluation by displacing responsibility for violent behavior, the probability of aggression and its maintenance is increased. Conditions of justification (Berkowitz & Rawlings, 1963; Brock & Buss, 1964; Meyer, 1972) and diffusion of responsibility (Bandura, Underwood, & Fromson, 1975) disinhibit the performance of aggressive actions. Corporate organizations appear designed to distribute responsibility in as many directions as possible (Sutherland, 1949). "The large corporation diffuses ever more important collective responsibilities among more and more people and separates ever more acts from consequences—the decision makers from those affected by the decisions. The buck seems to stop nowhere" (Mintz & Cohen, 1971, p. 295).

Depersonalization of Victims. When the victims of aggression are depersonalized, violent actions are facilitated. Milgram (1965) found that subjects are more willing to administer shock when they were less likely to see or be seen by the recipient of the shock. Reducing victim visibility was found to facilitate aggression in a naturalistic setting by Turner, Layton, and Simons (1975). Zimbardo (1969) and a recent study by Bandura, Underwood, and Fromson (1975) found that the dehumanization of victims increased aggressive behavior. To the extent that the consumers of hazardous products are removed in space and time from corporate decision makers, there exists a condition of anonymity that facilitates violence. Furthermore, when the victims are perceived to have voluntarily chosen a hazardous work environment, such as a coal mine, or a hazardous product, such as a Corvair, they can be seen by the decision makers to have invited their own misfortune.

STRATEGIES FOR RESEARCH ON CORPORATE CRIME

While the literature on aggression supplies some clues concerning the dynamics of corporate violence, strategies must be found to investigate its parameters more directly. At least three methods have promise for the study of corporate violence: the case study, naturalistic quasi-experimental research, and experimental laboratory simulations.

Case Studies

The intensive study of the individual case is one of the oldest research methods in social science. The failings of the case method—its lack of control and susceptibility to unwarranted generalization—are much better known than its contributions. In clinical work (Lazarus & Davison, 1971), as elsewhere, the detailed investigation of a single instance of a phenomenon has provided a wealth of data from which to generate hypotheses for experimental testing and has put flesh on theoretical abstractions. The case studies of corporate crime and corporate violence cited earlier have contributed substantially to our understanding of the subject. Further case studies are essential.

Naturalistic Quasi-Experimental Research

Research strategies that employ naturalistic data in a systematic manner are several steps up the ladder of methodological ascent from case studies. Campbell (1971) has detailed the strengths and the limitations of such approaches. Quasi-experimental designs appear to be particularly suited for studying corporate violence. In regard to the failure to recall defective automobiles, we found that two major Detroit auto manufacturers make recall decisions at the middle-management level, and two make such decisions at the top management level. Data from the National Highway Traffic Safety Administration—the federal agency that monitors recalls—reveals that in 1974, the latest year for which information is available, the two companies who used the middle-management decision makers were audited for safety violations a total of 10 times, while the two companies that make recall decisions at the top management level were audited only once. From this naturalistic data, one cannot infer that middle managers are more likely to take risks with the public safety than are persons at the top of the corporate structure. Many factors confound such a straightforward interpretation (e.g., differences in sales volume and financial status of the companies). But sophisticated use of naturalistic data in quasi-experimental research eventually may allow inferences on such questions to be drawn with a high degree of confidence.

Experimental Laboratory Simulations

As research students know, randomly assigned groups to control for various hypotheses are fundamental to "true" experimental methodology. Unfortunately, the conditions of the real world usually do not lend themselves to assignment by flipping a coin. This is clearly the case with corporate violence: defects and decision makers cannot be randomly assigned to experimental conditions. But if the laboratory cannot go to the corporation, perhaps the corporation can be brought to the laboratory. The technique of *laboratory simulation* has proved useful in other realms of psychological research, and may provide a method for studying corporate violence.

Simulation or "role playing" methods have been extensively used in psychological research (Freedman, 1969;
Greenberg, 1967; Kelman, 1967). Perhaps the best known
recent example of simulation research is the Stanford
Prison Experiment (Haney & Zimbardo, 1976). In this
study, college students played the role of either a prisoner
or a prison guard, and acted out various institutional rou-
tines. The study was terminated earlier than anticipated
because participants "got into" their roles so fully that
breakdowns and brutality that characterize a real prison
began to manifest themselves in the simulation. Research
on jury behavior also has relied heavily on simulation
methods (Tapp, 1976). While simulation research may at
times produce results quite unlike those obtained in the
natural situation (Ebbeson & Konecni, 1975) it also may
provide a highly useful analogue to situations otherwise
immune from experimental intrusions.

SIMULATION OF CORPORATE DECISION MAKING AND CORPORATE VIOLENCE

The following design and background data are presented as an example of a simulation strategy by which
the problem of corporate violence might be examined by
community psychologists. In this experimental scheme,
subjects would take the role of corporate officials who
make decisions that relate to consumer safety.

Automobile recalls represent the target problem. This
subject was selected for several reasons: (1) automobile
accidents are responsible for approximately 50,000 deaths
in the United States each year, a figure substantially
higher than the number of homicides (Department of
Transportation, 1976); (2) it is frequently alleged by consumer advocates that a substantial portion of these deaths
are attributable to the faulty manufacture of automobiles
(Nader, 1965); (3) recalling automobiles is the major industry response to discovered defects on marketed cars. Ap-

proximately two million American cars were recalled in 1975 in 190 separate recall orders (Department of Transportation, 1976); and (4) the corporate decision-making process in recalls appears particularly amenable to laboratory simulation.

Before designing the simulation, we sought to obtain a picture of how the decision to recall a car is made in the American automobile industry. We were surprised to find a total absence of published information on the topic, and even more surprised that none of the many sources we contacted in the Department of Transportation, in relevant Congressional committees, or in national consumer groups had any idea how the automobile industry went about making decisions on whether to recall an automobile. These groups were informed by the industry only after a corporate decision to recall had been made. Their knowledge of the recall process related only to the follow-up procedures mandated by the Highway Safety Acts of 1966 and 1973 (e.g., notification of owners) and the procedures whereby a company might be sued if it did not recall a car which the Department of Transportation determined to be a safety hazard. The absence of information concerning the internal corporate procedures that resulted in the original decision to recall or not recall forced us to look to the automobile industry itself for clues.

Interview Data from Automobile Corporations

Telephone interviews were conducted in February of 1976 with officials in Detroit of each of the "Big Four" American automobile manufacturers (Ford, General Motors, Chrysler, and American Motors). In each instance, the attempt was made to locate the persons in the company most knowledgeable about the decision to recall or not to recall automobiles. There was a substantial reluctance on the part of some persons we contacted to discuss company policy in this area. It was necessary on several occasions to assure the interviewee repeatedly that his comments were not being recorded and that he would remain anonymous. "Of course," said one middle-level executive after having described his corporation's procedures, "I'll categorically deny ever having talked to you."

To honor the guarantee of anonymity, the data are reported here only in summary fashion. In the case of two of the "Big Four," recall decisions are made by a top management committee. Information indicating the existence of a possible safety defect discovered by any part of the company (e.g., marketing, quality control, engineering) is forwarded to a *safety office* that is charged with coordinating data collection and soliciting supporting evidence. If the production department had discovered that the wrong bolt has been placed in the steering column of a given model car, for example, this information is sent to the safety office, which then commissions the engineering department to do stress tests on the new bolt and the service department to check repair records. The office collates the reports from the various departments and, in a cover memo, makes its own recommendation regarding a course of action (i.e., recall or not recall). The report is then sent to a *safety committee,* which in one case consists of 14 corporation vice-presidents (including the vice-presidents for public relations and for finance), and in the other consists of vice-presidents and members of the board of directors. This top management safety committee reviews the report and makes the final decision on whether or not to recall. If the decision is to recall, the safety office is directed to begin the notification of owners and the Department of Transportation.

The remaining two auto manufacturers employ a somewhat different procedure, with decisions in these companies made at lower levels in the organization. As in the first two companies, information regarding a safety defect may come from any department in the company. But, in these companies, there is no specific office charged with coordinating information. Rather, information is fed to a middle management *safety committee,* composed of approximately 18 people from the various departments (including finance and public relations). This committee reviews the evidence presented, and relevant members are told to solicit additional evidence from their departments (in the bolt example used earlier, the member from engineering would be told to obtain stress tests, and the member from finance would be told to come up with cost figures for a recall). This middle management committee reviews the evidence and makes a recommendation to "top management" on a course of action. There is no formal committee structure at the higher level in these two companies. If safety committee decision to recall is not vetoed by top management, the notification process begins.

Each of the "Big Four" auto manufacturers, therefore, has a safety committee that makes final or semi-final decisions on whether or not to recall. In two cases this committee is at the vice-president or board of directors level and works with material coordinated by a middle management safety office. In the other two cases, the safety committee is at the middle management level and is responsible for both coordinating the data and reaching a policy decision.

To simulate the actual decision-making process, a researcher might focus on a safety committee which makes its decisons on the reports gathered by a safety office. The subject population ideally would consist of corporate executives. This would substantially reduce problems of generalization associated with the more typical practice of employing college undergraduates. Subjects could be solicited from nearby industries or business school "executive education" classes and brought to an actual board room for a series of group tasks. They would be instructed to take the role of a member of an executive committee of a Detroit automobile manufacturer at a meeting called to consider a recall. Subjects would be presented with the reports from the safety office, instructed to discuss the merits of the case, and asked to vote on the recall decision. By manipulating the content of the reports, hypotheses derived from traditional psychological research on violence could be investigated.

The variables that a simulation strategy could explore include *decision costs* (Where on a continuum of costs to the corporation is a recall less likely to be ordered?); *possible sanctions* (Is recall more likely if exposure to lawsuits was likely to be severe as compared to slap-on-the-wrist?); *organizational setting* (Is a corporation in sound financial condition more likely to recall than one in a precarious financial state?); *decision makers* (Does the corporate level of the decision makers affect their decision to recall? Does the job function of the decision maker in the corporation affect his or her vote to recall?); and *probable victims* (Do characteristics of those persons who will be subject to a safety risk, such as their social class, affect recall decisions?).

CONCLUSIONS

We have argued that corporate violence is a significant social phenomenon and one which, for several reasons, has escaped psychological scrutiny. We have reviewed strategies for righting this research imbalance. Having emphasized scientific approaches to the problem of corporate violence in this chapter, we will conclude with a section from Arthur Miller's play, *All My Sons* (1947), which has as its protagonist a man who knowingly sold defective cylinder aircraft heads to the Army Air Force in World War II. Numerous plane crashes were caused by his act. Like many corporate offenders, he escaped conviction. At the end of the play, the man's son discovers his guilt, and the father tries to explain himself:

> I'm in a business, a man is in business; a hundred and twenty cylinder heads cracked, you're out of busi-

ness; you don't know how to operate, your stuff is no good; they close you up, they tear up your contracts, what the hell's it to them? You lay forty years into a business and they knock you out in five minutes, what could I do, let them take forty years, let them take my life away?

When told by his father that the cylinder heads were sold so that the business could be preserved for him, the son, who had been a pilot during the war, responds:

Where do you live, where have you come from? For me!—I was dying every day and you were killing my boys and you did it for me? What the hell do you think I was thinking of, the goddamn business? Is that as far as your mind can see, the business? What is that, the world—the business? What the hell do you mean, you did it for me? Don't you have a country? Don't you live in the world?

And, finally, when his mother asks him, "What more can we be!", the son responds: "You can be better! Once and for all you can know there's a universe of people outside and you're responsible to it."

Moralizing is not too fashionable these days, and perhaps Arthur Miller is a bit old-fashioned, but it seems reasonable that the lines he has the son utter ought to be kept in mind by community psychologists as they define their subject matter and conduct their research.

REFERENCES

Amir, M. *Patterns in forcible rape.* Chicago: University of Chicago Press, 1971.

Austin, W. T., & Bates, F. L. Ethological indicators of dominance and territoriality in a human captive population. *Social Forces,* 1974, *52,* 447–455.

Bandura, A. Influence of models' reinforcement contingencies on the acquisition of imitative responses. *Journal of Personality and Social Psychology*, 1965, *1*, 589–595.

Bandura, A. *Aggression: A social learning analysis.* Englewood Cliffs, N.J.: Prentice-Hall, 1973.

Bandura, A., Underwood, B., & Fromson, M. E. Disinhibition of aggression through diffusion of responsibility and dehumanization of victims. *Journal of Research in Personality*, 1975, *9*, 253–269.

Bard, M. The role of law enforcement in the helping system. In J. Monahan (Ed.), *Community Mental Health and the Criminal Justice System.* New York: Pergamon, 1976.

Baron, R. Exposure to an aggressive model and apparent probability of retaliation from the victim as determinants of adult aggressive behavior. *Journal of Experimental Social Psychology*, 1971, *1*, 343–355.

Baron, R., & Kemper, C. R. Model's behavior and attraction toward the model as determinants of adult aggressive behavior. *Journal of Personality and Social Psychology*, 1970, *14*, 335–344.

Baumhart, R. C. How ethical are businessmen? In G. Geis (Ed.), *White-Collar Criminal.* New York: Atherton, 1968.

Berkowitz, L. Some determinants of impulsive aggression: Role of mediated associations with reinforcements for aggression. *Psychological Review*, 1974, *81*, 165–176.

Berkowitz, L., & Rawlings, E. Effects of film violence on inhibitions against subsequent aggression. *Journal of Abnormal and Social Psychology*, 1963, *68*, 403–412.

Borgaonkar, D., & Shah, S. The XYY chromosome. In A. Steinberg and A. Bearne (Eds.), *Progress in medical genetics.* New York: Grune & Stratton, 1974, *10*, 135–222.

Brock, T. C., & Buss, A. Effects of justification for aggression and communication with the victim on post-aggression dissonance. *Journal of Abnormal and Social Psychology,* 1964, *68,* 403–412.

Brodeur, P. *Expendable Americans.* New York: Viking, 1974.

Buss, A. Physical aggression in relation to different frustrations. *Journal of Abnormal and Social Psychology,* 1963, *67,* 1–7.

Buss, A. Instrumentality of aggression, feedback, and frustration as determinants of physical aggression. *Journal of Personality and Social Psychology,* 1966, *3,* 153–162.

Campbell, D. Methods for the experimenting society. Unpublished manuscript, 1971.

Comstock, G. A., & Rubinstein, E. A. (Eds.) *Television and social behavior. Vol. III: Television and adolescent aggressiveness.* Washington, D.C.: U.S. Govt. Ptg. Off., 1972.

Department of Transportation. *Traffic safety '75.* Washington, D.C.: U.S. Gov't. Ptg. Off., 1976.

Ebbeson, E., & Konecni, V. Decision making and information integration in the courts: The setting of bail. *Journal of Personality and Social Psychology,* 1975, *32,* 805–821.

Einstadter, W. J. The social organization of armed robbery. *Social Problems,* 1969, *17,* 64–83.

Feshbach, S., & Singer, R. D. *Television and aggression.* San Francisco: Jossey-Bass, 1971.

Franklin, B. A. The scandal of death and injury in the mines. *New York Times Magazine,* March 30, 1969.

Freedman, J. Role playing: Psychology by consensus. *Journal of Personality and Social Psychology,* 1969, *13,* 107–114.

Geen, R. G., & Pigg, R. Acquisition of an aggressive response and its generalization to verbal behavior. *Journal of Personality and Social Psychology,* 1970, *15,* 165–170.

Geen, R. G., & Stonner, D. Effects of aggressive habit strength on behavior in the presence of aggression-related stimuli. *Journal of Personality and Social Psychology,* 1971, *17,* 149–153.

Geis, G. (Ed.) *White-collar criminal.* New York: Atherton, 1968.

Geis, G. Deterring corporate crime. In R. Nader, & M. Green (Eds.) *Corporate power in America.* New York: Grossman Publishing, 1973, pp. 182–197.

Geis, G., & Meier, R. *White-collar crime: Offenses in business, politics, and the professions.* New York: Free Press, 1977.

Geis, G., & Monahan, J. The social ecology of violence. In T. Lickona (Ed.), *Morality: Theory, research, and social issues.* New York: Holt, Rinehart, and Winston, 1976, pp. 342–356.

Greenberg, M. Role playing: An alternative to deception? *Journal of Personality and Social Psychology,* 1967, *1,* 152–157.

Halleck, S. A multidimensional approach to violence. In D. Chappell & J. Monahan (Eds.), *Violence and criminal justice.* Lexington, Mass.: Lexington Books, 1975.

Haney, C., & Zimbardo, P. The socialization into criminality: On becoming a prisoner and a guard. In J. Tapp, & F. Levine (Eds.), *Law, Justice and the Individual in Society.* New York: Holt, Rinehart, and Winston, 1976.

Hartmann, D. P. Influence of symbolically modeled instrumental aggression and pain cues on aggressive behavior. *Journal of Personality and Social Psychology,* 1969, *11,* 280–288.

Ittleson, W., Proshansky, H., Rivlin, L., & Winkel, G. *An introduction to environmental psychology.* New York: Holt, Rinehart, and Winston, 1974.

Johnson, R. *Aggression in man and animals.* Philadelphia: W. B. Saunders, 1972.

Kelman, H. C. Human use of human subjects: The problem of deception in psychological experiments. *Psychological Bulletin,* 1967, *67,* 1–11.

Lane, R. Why businessmen violate the law. *Journal of*

Criminal Law, Criminology, and Police Science, 1953, *44*, 151–165.

Lazarus, A., & Davison, G. Clinical innovation in research and practice. In A. Bergin, & S. Garfield (Eds.), *Handbook of psychotherapy and behavior change*. New York: Wiley, 1971.

Meyer, T. Effects of viewing justified and unjustified real film violence on aggressive behavior. *Journal of Personality and Social Psychology*, 1972, *22*, 21–29.

Milgram, S. Behavioral study of obedience. *Journal of Abnormal and Social Psychology*, 1963, *67*, 371–378.

Milgram, S. Some conditions of obedience and disobedience to authority. *Human Relations*, 1965, *18*, 57–76.

Miller, A. *All My Sons.* New York: Dramatists Play Service, 1947.

Mintz, M., & Cohen, J. S. *America, inc.* New York: Dial Press, 1971.

Monahan, J. The prevention of violence. In J. Monahan (ed.), *Community mental health and the criminal justice system.* New York: Pergamon Press, 1976, pp. 14–41.

Moyer, K. E. The physiological inhibition of hostile behavior. In J. F. Knutson (Ed.), *The control of aggression.* Chicago: Aldine, 1973.

Nader, R. *Unsafe at any speed.* New York: Grossman Publishers, 1965.

Novaco, R. W. *Anger control: The development and evaluation of an experimental treatment.* Lexington, Mass.: D.C. Heath, Lexington Books, 1975.

Novaco, R. W. A stress inoculation approach to anger management in the training of law enforcement officers. *American Journal of Community Psychology*, 1977, 5, 327–346.

Office of Management and Budget. *Social indicators.* Washington D.C.: U.S. Gov't. Ptg. Off., 1973.

Quinney, R. *A critique of legal order.* Boston: Little, Brown, 1974.

Sutherland, E. H. *White collar crime*. New York: Holt, Rinehart, and Winston, 1949.

Tapp, J. Psychology and the law: An overture. *Annual Review of Psychology*, 1976, *27*, 258–404.

Turner, C. W., Layton, J. F., & Simons, L. S. Naturalistic studies of aggressive behavior: Aggressive stimuli, victim visibility, and horn honking. *Journal of Personality and Social Psychology*, 1975, *31*, 1098–1107.

Vallenstein, E. *Brain control*. New York: Wiley Interscience, 1974.

Wolfgang, M. E. *Patterns in criminal homicide*. Philadelphia: University of Pennsylvania Press, 1958.

Wolfgang, M. E., & Ferracuti, F. *The subculture of violence*. London: Travistock, 1971.

Zimbardo, P. G. The human choice: Individuation, reason, and order versus deindividuation, impulse, and chaos. *Nebraska Symposium on Motivation, 1969*. Lincoln, Nebraska: 1969, 237–309.

6. The Psychology of Evil, or The Perversion of Human Potential*

PHILIP G. ZIMBARDO

Making use of observations in the contemporary world, Zimbardo contributes a thought-provoking essay. His is a convincing argument that all of us are potential malefactors and benefactors, and that all of us are potential clients of criminal justice systems. Zimbardo's chapter serves as a coda for this volume. Although it is an independent contribution, it underscores and illuminates the conclusions of the other contributors. Crime and justice can no longer be perceived as something that happens to "them." In one way or another, we are all participants in the criminal justice system.

It is the human capacity for justice that makes the rule of law possible, but it is the human capacity for evil that makes law necessary.

A basic theme in Western thought is that man—once great, once the most noble paragon of all creatures—has suffered a great fall from his state of perfection. In *Gulliver's Travels,* the king of the Brobdingnags levels a total

*Reprinted by permission from "The Psychology of Evil: or the Perversion of Human Potential," by Philip G. Zimbardo, Ph.D., in vol. 4, *Advances in the Study of Communications and Affect Aggression, Dominance, and Individual Spacing,* L. Krames, P. Pliner, and T. Alloway (Eds.) (Plenum Press, New York, 1978).

condemnation of the human race against Gulliver during his travels:

> [The historical account of humans is a] heap of conspiracies, rebellions, murders, massacres, revolutions, banishments, the very worst effects that avarice, faction, hypocrisy, perfidiousness, cruelty, rage, madness, hatred, envy, lust, malice, and ambition could produce.
>
> ... I cannot but conclude the bulk of your natives to be the most pernicious race of little odious vermin that nature ever suffered to crawl upon the surface of the earth [Jonathan Swift, *Gulliver's Travels*, 1726, Pt. 2, Ch. 6].

Accepting this human propensity for evil,[1] it has remained for theologians, philosophers, social scientists, and legislators to debate the origins of that evil. Are we, as Rousseau envisioned, noble, primitive savages born in God-like innocence only to be corrupted by contact with society? Standing in stark opposition to this general view of human beings as the innocent victims of an all-powerful, malignant society is the view that people are basically evil. According to this view, people are driven by desires, appetites, and impulses unless they are transformed into rational, reasonable, compassionate human beings by education, or controlled by the firm authority of the home, church, or state institutions.

Where do *you* stand in this argument? Are we born good and corrupted by an evil society, or born evil and

[1] *Evil* is a term applied to "situations when force, violence, and other forms of coercion exceed institutional or moral limits" (Smelser, 1971). The three classes of situations that qualify as "evil" by this definition are those in which individuals or groups: (1) exercise coercive power over others when they are not legitimately empowered to do so; (2) exceed the limits of their legitimate authority to exercise coercion; or (3) exercise coercive or destructive control over others that violates a higher standard of humanity or morality even though it may be within politically sanctioned authority.

redeemed by a good society? And do you believe that evil deeds flow from the evil motives of people who are basically "evil" (like *them*), while goodness is a quality that is inherent in certain other people (perhaps like *you*)? Before casting your ballot, consider an alternative perspective. Maybe each of us has the capacity to be a saint or a sinner, altruistic or selfish, gentle or cruel, dominant or submissive, sane or mad, prisoner or guard. Maybe it is the social circumstances we experience and how we learn to cope with them that determine which potential we develop. In fact, maybe the potential for perversion is inherent in the very processes that make us able to do all the superbly wonderful things we can do.

For untold millions of years of evolution and adaptation, we have become the rulers of this planet, controlling the other animals and the physical matter of the earth for our survival, comfort, and happiness. This reign is currently being extended to life beneath the oceans as well as to outer space. We have reached this position because of our capacity for learning new and remembering old relationships, for reasoning, inventing, and planning action strategies. We have developed language to manipulate symbols and transmit our thoughts and information to others. But each of these unique attributes can also become cancerous. The seeds of our perversion are nourished in the soil of the human potential for perfectibility.

For example, our remarkable memory enables us to profit from mistakes, establish continuities within our lives, and master complex feats of learning. But this same gift of memory can convert our minds into storehouses filled with traumatic events, fears, anxieties, unresolved conflicts, and petty grudges. Our capacity for love allows us to experience the most tender and subtle of emotions, to feel special and needed, to nurture the growth of our beloved and to sacrifice for their well-being. But love can also lead to jealousy, possessiveness, domination, obsession, and its loss to depression, revenge, and suicide.

Because we have developed a unique temporal per-

spective, we can plan for our fu
day," delay gratification, and pro
cause of this very sense of time
often loses its spontaneity. We fa
the love others offer or the joy
through each day's obligations,
ments (our *past* contracts), while
avoiding liabilities, and anticipati
concerns).

Without the human conceptic... ... ...
sense there could be no hope, but there would also be no
guilt.

EMPIRICAL RESEARCH ON EVIL

For the past ten years I have been engaged in research
at New York University and now at Stanford University
(funded by the Office of Naval Research) studying violence, vandalism, and other forms of antisocial behavior.
My colleagues and I have not only tried to systematically
observe these forms of evil as they exist in everyday life,
but in addition, we have attempted to manipulate evil,
creating it as well as preventing it under carefully controlled laboratory conditions.

The general conclusion that emerges from this body of
research runs contrary to prevailing stereotypes that locate the source of evil *in people.* Rather, these investigations have led me to accept the wisdom of Nathaniel
Hawthorne's assertion that, "There is no such thing in
man's nature as a settled and free resolve either for good
or evil, except at the very moment of execution" [*Twice
Told Tales,* 1837]. In addition, I will argue in favor of a
conception of evil as a behavioral act that is best understood in terms of the prevailing social conditions that
elicit it and the situational forces that instigate and encourage it.

Before I describe some of the evidence which supports

—and in the process, describe how easy it is to
ood people engage in evil acts—it is necessary first
onsider why we all prefer to find *people* who are
rsonally responsible for the evil we see all around us
rather than *situations* that are causally responsible for it.

We have been programmed by our socialization process
and basic institutions to accept doctrines of *individual*
guilt, sin, culpability, and failure, as well as to accept the
cult of the ego, the strength of character, and the stability
of personality.

This egocentric orientation assumes that there is in
each of us a stable core of values, beliefs, attitudes, and a
constellation of personality traits that guide and rationally
direct our behavior. Defects in behavior are therefore
traceable to defects within the person. Defects within the
person who breaks laws, or violates the rules are then
evidence of a psychopathic, sociopathic, or deviant personality or character disorder. Or at a simpler level, such
people are the sinners, the criminals, the bad guys.

Dispositional versus Situational Attribution

Who is to blame? *Who* is responsible? *Who* must pay
for the damages? *Who* must be punished? This question
is purposely phrased in this way as *who,* and not as *what*
is to blame? *What* is responsible and *how* can we change
the undesirable behavior knowing *what* are its causes.
These two approaches are the *dispositional* and the *situational.* The analysis of social problems—crime, violence,
riots, rebellion, wars, vandalism, poverty, sexual abandon
—according to those who espouse a dispositional orientation always locates "the problem" inside the person. Evil
is in the soul, spirit, heart, head, guts of the evil doer.
There are three primary reasons why such a view is so
readily accepted and so resistant to challenge.

First, it assumes that the evil doer is different from the
rest of us in fundamental ways, since he or she did the evil

deed and we have not. Therefore, we need not identify with him or her, feel empathy towards, nor share the guilt of such a person. It also allows us to feel superior by virtue of this difference between "us" (as the good) and "them" (as the bad). We thus distance ourselves and make the evil act and its perpetrator alien to us.

Second, we need not feel responsible for having created or perpetuated social, economic, political, or psychological conditions that may have caused the evil behavior, since by *assuming* an internal origin of the act, external causation is irrelevant or merely an extenuating circumstance. Our analysis is thus simplified as well as our guilt assuaged.

Third, by holding this "evil seed" theory of behavior, or by believing that some people who commit deeds we label as "evil" are "incorrigible," then it follows that their behavior cannot be modified, and so we do not have to really try to save them, or change them or change the conditions surrounding the evil act. The solution is again simple, *instead of* recognizing the particular, complex circumstances associated with the act and then determining an individualized treatment, or the need to make basic changes in the quality of life, we take note of the evil *in* the evildoer and prescribe institutional isolation, segregation, punishment, or extermination. Paradoxically it is by personalizing evil that we are able to deal with it in an impersonal manner.

One message of contemporary social psychology is that we all *overestimate* the extent to which behavior—be it evil, good, or neuter—is *dispositionally controlled,* while at the same time we systematically *underestimate* the degree to which it is *situationally controlled.* We walk around with the soothing illusion of personal invulnerability, of our inner strength to resist temptation and evil, fortified by our strong moral fiber. We are convinced that good people triumph in evil situations, thus evil must not be in the power of certain situations to corrupt and pervert any of us, but in evil people. It is precisely this attributional error that makes us most vulnerable to evil influences. Some selected discomforting thoughts on this are listed here:

1. It is not possible to predict with any certainty how a given person will behave in a particular situation solely from knowledge of his/her personality, however it is assessed.
2. No one can reliably predict violence from so-called measures of proneness to violence in individual cases.
3. Because you may not *yet* have committed an evil deed, you cannot be sure you will not do so in the future if you are put into particular kinds of situations.
4. It is likely that you have committed evil in the past and that you are currently doing so, although you do not define the acts in question as evil.
5. Evil is typically in the eye of the observer, it is never in the mind of the doer.
6. Under the appropriate circumstances, any one could be a potential assassin or a potential victim.
7. The setting for evil is rarely dramatic, evil operates most often when it is trivial and banal, routinized and sanforized.

Let us now examine the basis for such apparently cynical views.

THE BANALITY OF EVIL

Last year more San Franciscans killed each other than ever before. Troubled by this record-breaking evil, the San Francisco Police Department set about to analyze the motives for the 131 homicides. The principal motive was "a trivial argument" (the second most frequent motive being sex). Representative of these trivial triggering incidents were: stepping on a man's foot at a party, missing a billiard shot, taking someone's seat and having mustard instead of the requested catsup put on a steak. But someone died because of such "evil" motivations, that someone was usually a white male shot to death by a friend or relative.

In a quite different context, Hannah Arendt (1965) concluded from her observations of the war crimes' trial of Adolph Eichmann that despite the enormity of the holocaust in the Nazi concentration camps, the operation of evil itself was in its day-to-day manifestation rather banal. Petty bureaucrats following orders, signing death certificates, meeting quotas, trying to please superiors, not wanting to offend, and above all, concerned about doing their duty and being obedient.

Could *you* send a Jew to a gas chamber? Could *you* electrocute a perfect stranger because someone asked you to? Is it not comforting to think of the horrors of Nazi Germany as the evil of another time, a different place, and a peculiar Germanic character that thrives on authoritarian obedience? It could never happen here, not now, by Americans, and certainly not by you! It is sad to say there is compelling evidence that it could, and that *you* would.

BLIND OBEDIENCE TO AUTHORITY

Stanley Milgram contrived a situation in which subjects believed they were shocking a stranger as part of a study of the effects of punishment on learning. Whenever the learner made an error, the teacher-subject was instructed to press a lever that would deliver an electric shock to the middle-aged learner. The subjects were Yale students as well as businessmen and ordinary citizens from Bridgeport, Connecticut. The special feature of this study was that the level of punishment escalated by 15 volts for each successive error. The shock generator had 30 levers from

15 volts all the way up to 450 volts where it was marked "Danger, severe shock." The protests of the victim, heard over an intercom, rose with the shock level being administered. At 75 volts he began to moan and grunt; at 150 volts he demanded to be released from the experiment; at 180 volts he cried out that he could not stand the pain any longer. At 300 volts he insisted that he would no longer take part in the experiment and must be freed. He yelled out about his heart condition, screamed, and then failed to respond at all over the last series of trials.

If the subject hesitated or protested against delivering the next shock, the experimenter told him, "Teacher, you have no other choice; you must go on!" "Your job is to punish the learner's mistakes." The experimenter insisted that absence of a response must also be punished, because the *rule* stated that this was to be considered an error.

The situation was not an enjoyable one for the subjects, in fact, it produced considerable anguish in many. To shock an innocent stranger at such high voltage levels obviously was an act of extreme violence against another human being. Most subjects complained and protested. As they became alarmed that they might even kill the learner if one of their shocks caused him to have a heart attack, they insisted they could not go on with their job. That the experimental situation produced considerable conflict is readily apparent from a sample of the transcript given here:

> 180 volts delivered: 'He can't stand it! I'm not going to kill that man in there! You hear him hollering? He's hollering. He can't stand it. What if something happens to him? . . . I mean who is going to take the responsibility if anything happens to that gentleman?' [The experimenter accepts responsibility.] 'All right.'
>
> 195 volts delivered: 'You see he's hollering. Hear that. Gee, I don't know.' [The experimenter says: 'The experiment requires that you go on.']—'I know

it does, sir, but I mean—huh—he don't know what
he's in for. He's up to 195 volts. . . .'
  240 volts delivered: 'Aw, no. You mean I've got to
keep going up with that scale? No sir, I'm not going
to kill that man! I'm not going to give him 450 volts!'
[1965, p. 67]

The majority of the subjects, like this one, dissented *but
they did not disobey.* Nearly two thirds of the subjects (62
percent) kept pressing the levers all the way to the very
last switch that delivered 450 volts, the maximum punishment possible! When the study was repeated using high
school students tested with an authority figure who had
considerable prestige telling them they must continue, a
remarkable 85% went all the way.

Personality tests did not reveal any differences between
those people who refused to comply and the majority who
showed total, blind obedience to authority. You will recall
that there was a similar failure to find any individual
differences between American POWs in the Korean War
who collaborated with their Chinese captors and those
who resisted.

In these studies those situational forces are identified as:
the presence of a "legitimate" authority who assumes responsibility for the consequences of one's actions; a victim
who is physically remote; acceptance of a subordinate role
with functions governed by rules; and finally allowing
oneself to become part of a social system where public
etiquette and protocol are more important to maintain
than one's personal values and private beliefs.

An experiment such as this one is valuable not only
because it provides answers, but also because it raises new
questions and compels us to rethink some of our assumptions about human nature. It shatters the myth that evil
is alien to Everyman and Everywoman and lurks only in
particular other people who are different from us. It is a
convincing demonstration that the "Eichmann phenomenon" could be reproduced in the majority of ordinary

American citizens under specifiable social conditions. We do not like to believe such truths; we defend against them by saying it was "just an experiment," it's not "real life." But C. P. Snow (1961) reminds us:

> When you think of the long and gloomy history of man, you will find more hideous crimes have been committed in the name of obedience than have been committed in the name of rebellion.

OBEDIENCE IN REAL WORLD SETTINGS

No one was really hurt in Milgram's experiment because the victim was actually a confederate, but consider the following real-life analogue in an interview I had with a veteran from Vietnam, who was a medical corpsman:

> *Veteran:* My last two weeks there in the jungle we're on a routine patrol and this little girl about three years old starts running toward us. She was about forty or sixty feet away from us at the time, we noticed something bouncing on her back as she ran, and our officer said "shoot." We shot her down. At the same time we shot her down she exploded. She blew into small bits. The V.C. attached a savoy mine to her back and it was wired to explode by the time she reached us. It was either her or us. We didn't know for sure the mine was there but we couldn't take the chance.
> *Zimbardo:* When the officer said "shoot," how many people shot?
> *Veteran:* We all shot at her. There was about thirty of us in this particular platoon.
> *Zimbardo:* But did *you* have to do it?
> *Veteran:* Right. You have to do it, you are ordered to do it. You either shoot them, or if you don't shoot them, your officer shoots you. You don't have any choice. No choice about it, you don't have time to think about it, you do it.

Obedience is a virtue we instill in our children, but when it becomes perverted into blind, unquestioning obedience to authority, then it may give rise to the evil deeds of an Eichmann, or of President Nixon's inner circle who preferred to call it "loyalty to the Chief" rather than Eichman's obedience to his dictator.

ANONYMITY AND AGGRESSION

But to make people act aggressively against one another it is not necessary to have them knuckle under to an authority figure. In an experiment I conducted with mild mannered co-eds from New York University, simply putting them in a group and making them feel anonymous—no one knew who they were or cared—was sufficient to reduce their inhibitions against aggression. The anonymous girls who were hooded and in a darkened room delivered twice as much shock to other girl-victims as did the groups of girls who were made to feel identifiable.

In other studies in different parts of the country it has been shown that anonymity increases the likelihood of stealing and cheating as well as of aggression. Treating other people as if they were impersonal objects and making them feel anonymous sets the occasion for a wide range of antisocial behavior in normally law-abiding people.

VANDALISM

But anonymity is not something psychologists invented, it has become a characteristic of life in our cities. It is so much a part of the everyday scene in a place like New York City that even without hoods over their heads, people realize they are anonymous strangers to virtually everyone else they pass on the streets. We wondered whether this pervasive anonymity would make it more likely for people to vandalize abandoned automobiles in New York City, than say in Palo Alto, where there is still a sense of community. We were also curious about *who* vandals were; we assumed they were irresponsible youngsters, probably from lower class, minority groups. To test our preconceptions, Scott Fraser and I (Zimbardo, 1969) did a simple study; cars were abandoned near New York University and Stanford and hidden cameras recorded what happened to them.

The car in New York was subject to 23 separate attacks by vandals in three days and was finally reduced to a battered, useless pile of junk. The first attackers drove up in a new car and appeared to be a father, mother, and small son. They removed the radiator, battery, and contents of the glove compartment and trunk. All of the vandals were white, well-dressed adults, (except for a single group of young children) who under other circumstances would be identified as typical, middle-class advocates of greater law and order. In Palo Alto the abandoned car was not even touched in a week, although as many people passed it by.

THE EVIL OF INACTION

There is more to this demonstration than that New York's greater anonymity allows for more vandalism than in California. During the act of vandalism against this valuable property not one passerby interceded in any way to complain or censure the vandals. Is this failure to act not itself a sanction of evil?

When thousands of Japanese-Americans were rounded up in the state of California in 1941 and herded into concentration camps in the southwestern deserts, how many Americans condoned this action by silence? And how many were convinced that the "yellow menace" was a real threat to national security? But no one herded German- or Italian-Americans into such camps on the east coast where the threat was at least as great, if not more so.

The eloquent works of Elie Wiesel (1969, 1970) speak of the evil of silence when he described his experiences at Auschwitz which left him wondering not at the cruelty of his captors, but at the evil of all those neighbors who watched and saw and never intervened, and then psychologically denied the very existence of the concentration camps.

From a recent study at Princeton University we learn that one of the reasons we do not help a fellow in distress is not because we have grown callous, but simply because we don't have time, we're in too much of a hurry. In this study by Darley and Batson, (1973) theology students were on their way to deliver a sermon on the parable of the Good Samaritan. Some of them had been told by the experimenters they were late, others that they had time. The situation was rigged so that each theology student came across a man who was lying in an alleyway moaning and covered with blood. Here was a chance to practice what they were about to preach. But did they? Only 10 percent of those in a hurry to give the Good Samaritan sermon stopped to aid a victim in distress! The more time they thought they had, the more likely they were to stop. However, when asked later why they did not stop, the theologians did come up with an interesting variety of justifications.

JUSTIFYING EVIL DEEDS

One of the greatest contributors to both the evil of action and the evil of inaction, is our limitless imagination that can generate justifications for virtually any action.

Historically, collective violence has flowed regularly out of the central, political processes of Western countries. Men seeking to seize, hold, or realign the levers of power have continually engaged in collective violence as part of their struggles. The oppressed have struck in the name of justice, the privileged in the name of order, those in between in the name of fear [Tilly, 1969, pp. 4–5].

People who violate basic laws of humanity often are convinced that evil is about to be wrought on *them.* Typically, they rationalize their behavior according to some principle acceptable to others in their society. In addition, they often have some degree of social or political support or institutionalized structure that helps make it possible to redefine the act in other than its human terms. Consider Hitler's justification in *Mein Kampf:*

Thus, if we review all the causes of the German collapse, the final and decisive one is seen to be the failure to realize the racial problem and, more especially, the Jewish menace. . . . Thus do I now believe that I must act in the sense of the Almightly Creator: by fighting against the Jews I am doing the Lord's work [1933, p. 25].

Consider the reason mass killer Herbert Mullin gave for killing four teenage boys in Santa Cruz, California in 1973: He "punished" the "hippies" because they influenced him to be a conscientious objector and not to be a soldier "in the best country on earth." He also killed thirteen people in the belief that their human sacrifice would prevent a catastrophic earthquake (Associated Press, August 7, 1973). Here again is the paradox of human perfection—the same mind that can comprehend the most profound philosophical and metaphysical truths can distort reality so that "evil" becomes "good."

THE EVIL OF ROLES AND RULES IN A PRISON

In a mock prison we (Craig Haney, Curt Banks, and I) (Haney, Banks, & Zimbardo, 1973) created at Stanford a situation in which college students from throughout the country behaved in pathological ways within a few days after playing the roles of prisoners or guards in a realistic prison setting. The guards behaved brutally, often sadistically, and the prisoners, after an initial rebellion, were docile and compliant, but half of them became so psychologically disturbed they had to be released prematurely. The guards readily justified their aggression by pointing to the threats posed by the greater number of inmates than guards, their treachery, the need to show them who was boss, and so on. When the planned two-week study had to be terminated after only five days, the guards were amazed to recall how alien their behavior was to their usual selves. "I couldn't tell where I ended and my role began" said one of our meanest guards. "I treated the prisoners like cattle and believed we had to watch them closely or they would not follow the rules or try to attack us," said another student who totally got into his new role as prison guard.

THE FINAL SOLUTION REVISITED

To study just how easy it is to get people to endorse the final solution of genocide for so-called unfit people, a former student of mine, Helge Mansson, and his colleagues at the University of Hawaii tested over 1000 students in the following study (1972). A brief speech was given about the impending danger of overpopulation by mentally and physically unfit peoples. The audience was flattered at being chosen to assist the government in determining how to deal with this "problem" because they were intelligent, educated, and had high ethical values. After the speech opinions were solicited concerning the final solution. The results were that 90% agreed that there will always be people who are more fit to survive than others; 91% agreed that "it is entirely just to eliminate those judged dangerous to the general welfare"; 85% preferred to assist only with the decisions of who should be killed; while 8% preferred to assist directly with the killings.

Most surprisingly, nearly a third of the students even supported the final solution when applied to their own families, only if necessary, of course!

BUSINESS AS USUAL

Many people would not believe that they would be involved in the above described evil. However, in business this does occur. Tax evasion, price-fixing, and misleading advertising are examples of more "legitimized" violence; they are usually tolerated by the general public, either through ignorance of what is going on or because such activities are less personally threatening than what people see as "real" crime, such as robbery, muggings, and rape. In a classic study (Sutherland, 1949, 1968), the seventy largest industrial and commercial corporations in the United States were all found to have engaged in illegal activities. All of them had been prosecuted for various crimes, with the average company receiving 14 convictions. Given this high rate of recidivism, 90 percent of these companies could be legally considered habitual criminals. The people who engage in this kind of crime, however, do not feel they are doing something really wrong:

> Businessmen differ from professional thieves principally in their greater interest in status and respectability. They think of themselves as honest men, not as criminals, whereas professional thieves, when they speak honestly, admit they are thieves. The businessman does regard himself as a lawbreaker, but he thinks the laws are wrong or at least that they should not restrict him, although they may well restrict others. He does not think of himself as a criminal, because he does not conform to the popular stereotype

of the criminal. This popular stereotype is always taken from the lower socioeconomic class [Sutherland, 1968].

This sort of attitude toward crime may be the reason why some people, such as a former governor of California, felt the participants in the Watergate conspiracy should not be punished because "they weren't criminal types."

AN OPTIMISTIC CONCLUSION AFTER ALL THAT?

After all these years of being surrounded by the ugliness of evil in my research and observation, I still remain an optimist precisely because I believe that collectively we can change the situations, environments, and experiences that give rise to the perversion of human perfection. We must begin however, by not seeking the simplistic refuge of the dispositional analysis, the *who* question. Instead we should encourage understanding of the *what* and *how* of crime, violence and vandalism. Evil, however you define it, is a complex process that requires complex solutions, but they can be found in the type of situational variables I have tried to show elicit evil so readily.

The reader is urged to question illegitimate authority. If you dissent because of your moral principles be willing also to disobey. Do not allow yourself to be forced into roles of power where that power can be abused. Do not allow secrecy in the operation of government nor in our institutions, especially our prisons. Make other people feel wanted, recognized, and worthwhile. Make the time to help someone in distress, look at your own possibly evil actions not from a self-justifying perspective, but from that of someone else, say Judge Sirica's perspective. Do not reject people because they are different from you in appearance or ideas, instead try to appreciate the basis for that difference. Finally, and most important, I encourage you to help prevent evil by promoting the old-fashioned virtues of neighborhood and community values. You alone can prevent or reduce crime by showing you care about others who might commit a crime against you. And as I have tried to show, *we are all potential assassins,* so I ask for your recognition and love, and in turn, am willing to give them to you, both from fear of the evil that can result from not doing so, and from anticipation of the joys that such shared trust can bring to each of us.

REFERENCES

Arendt, H. *Eichmann in Jerusalem: A report on the banality of evil.* New York: Viking, 1965.

Darley, J. M., & Batson, C. O. From Jerusalem to Jericho: A study of situational variables in helping behavior. *Journal of Personality and Social Psychology,* 1973, *27,* 100–108.

Haney, C., Banks, C., & Zimbardo, P. Interpersonal dynamics in a simulated prison. *International Journal of Criminology and Penology,* 1973, *1,* 69–97.

Hawthorne, N. *Twice Told Tales,* 1837.

Hitler, A. *My Battle,* E. T. S. Dugdale (Trans.). New York: Houghton Mifflin, 1933.

Mansson, H. H. Justifying the final solution. *Omega, 3* (2), 1972, 79–87.

Snow, C. P. Either-or. *Progressive,* 1961, *25* (2), 24–25.

Sutherland, E. H. *White collar crime.* New York: Holt, Rinehart and Winston, 1949.

Sutherland, E. H. Crime of corporations. In G. Geis (Ed.), *White collar criminal.* New York: Atherton, 1968.

Tilly, C. Collective violence in the European perspective. In H. D. Graham and T. R. Gurr (Eds.), *Violence in America: Historical and comparative perspectives.* New York: New American Library, 1969.

Wiesel, E. *Night.* New York: Avon Books, 1969.

Wiesel, E. *The town beyond the wall.* New York: Avon Books, (Bard Ed.), 1970.

Zimbardo, P. G. The human choice: Individuation, reason, and order versus deindividuation, impulse, and chaos. In W. J. Arnold and D. Levine (Eds.), *1969 Nebraska symposium on motivation.* Lincoln, Nebraska: University of Nebraska Press, 1970, 237–307.

Index

164 Index